Cambridge English

MINDSET

FOR IELTS

An Official Cambridge IELTS Course

Cambridge University Press

www.cambridge.org/elt

Cambridge English Language Assessment

www.cambridgeenglish.org

www.cambridge.org
Information on this title: www.cambridge.org/9781316636688

First published 2017

20 19 18 17 16 15 14 13 12 11 10 9 8 7 6 5 4

Printed in Great Britain by CPI Group (UK) Ltd, Croydon CRO 4YY

A catalogue record for this publication is available from the British Library

Additional resources for this publication at www.cambridge.org/mindsetforielts

CONTENTS

MEET THE AUTHORS

With a thorough understanding of the essential skills required to succeed in the IELTS test, let our team of experts guide you on your IELTS journey.

Greg Archer

Greg Archer is an experienced, DELTA-qualified teacher and teacher trainer who began teaching *IELTS* at International House in London, where he trained and qualified as an *IELTS* Examiner in both Writing and Speaking. After moving to Cambridge in 2013, he has been working at an international college, at various times managing the English Language department, developing appropriate courses to run alongside A Level and GCSE study, and primarily teaching *IELTS* and English for Academic Purposes classes to students whose ambition is to enter a UK or English-speaking university.

Lucy Passmore

Lucy began teaching English in 2002 in the UK and Spain, where she prepared young learners for Cambridge English exams. She has been a tutor of English for Academic Purposes since 2008, and has taught on *IELTS* preparation courses in addition to preparing international students to start degree courses at Brunel University and King's College London. Lucy is currently based at King's College London, where she teaches on foundation programmes for international students, provides in-sessional support in academic writing for current students and contributes to materials and course design.

The *Mindset for IELTS* authors have extensive experience teaching in the UK and globally. They have helped prepare students for the *IELTS* test from all over the world, including:

China, UK, Pakistan, Middle East, Republic of Korea, Italy, Indonesia, Sri Lanka, Kazakhstan, Greece, Russia, Spain

Peter Crosthwaite

Peter has worked in the TESOL and applied linguistics fields for 13 years. His previous experience includes writing and consultancy work with various publishers, two sessions as Director of Studies for language schools in the UK, over six years' experience in the Korean EFL context, and teaching and supervision experience at the University of Cambridge. He is currently an Assistant Professor at the Centre for Applied English Studies (CAES), University of Hong Kong, where he is the coordinator of the MA Applied Linguistics (MAAL) and the MA TESOL. He is currently co-teaching the 'Second Language Acquisition' module for both programs. He has worked on *IELTS* test preparation, publishing and materials development for over 10 years, with 4 years of experience as a qualified *IELTS* Examiner.

Natasha De Souza

Natasha has been involved in the ELT industry for 15 years – as a teacher, Director of Studies, Examiner and an Examinations Officer. She started teaching *IELTS* in 2006, when she worked on a University Pathway and Foundation Programme for a language school in Cambridge. More recently, as a Director of Studies and an Examinations Officer, she was responsible for giving guidance to students and teachers on how the *IELTS* test works and how best to prepare for it.

Jishan Uddin

Jishan has been an EFL teacher since 2001. He has taught on a range of courses in the UK and Spain, including general English, exam preparation and English for Academic Purposes (EAP) courses and is currently an EAP lecturer and academic module leader at King's College, London. He has extensive experience teaching *IELTS* preparation classes to students from around the world, particularly China, the Middle East and Kazakhstan. He also has experience in designing resources for language skills development as well as exam preparation and administration.

Susan Hutchison

Susan Hutchison has been an ESOL teacher and examiner for more than 30 years. She has taught overseas in Italy, Hungary and Russia. She now lives and works in Edinburgh, Scotland as an ESOL teacher in an independent school for girls. She has co-authored a number of course books, preparation and practice materials for both Cambridge English Language Assessment and *IELTS*. She has also developed online and interactive *IELTS* practice materials for the British Council.

Marc Loewenthal

Marc has been teaching for 35 years, mostly in the UK but also abroad in Greece, Russia, Middle East, Indonesia and Pakistan. He has taught in the public sector since 1990, mostly in further education and adult education, and more recently on pre-sessional EAP university courses. He has been a Speaking and Writing Examiner for over 25 years and has expert knowledge of *IELTS* requirements for university admission.

Claire Wijayatilake

Claire has been teaching English since 1988. She spent much of her career in Sri Lanka, including 16 years at British Council, Colombo. She became an *IELTS* Examiner in 1990 and examined regularly in Colombo and Malé, Maldives for almost 20 years. She worked as the *IELTS* Examiner Trainer for Sri Lanka, recruiting, training and monitoring examiners. She then moved into training and school leadership, serving as Teacher Trainer and Principal at various international schools. She returned to the UK in 2013 and worked for Middlesex University, where she started her materials writing career. She is currently a Visiting Lecturer at Westminster University, which allows her time to write. She has a PhD in Applied Linguistics and English Language Teaching from the University of Warwick.

HOW DOES MINDSET FOR IELTS WORK?

AVAILABLE AT FOUR LEVELS

| FOUNDATION LEVEL | LEVEL 1 Target Band 5.5 | LEVEL 2 Target Band 6.5 | LEVEL 3 Target Band 7.5 |

CORE MATERIAL

- Student's Book (print and digital).
- Online skills modules for Reading, Writing, Listening, Speaking plus Grammar and Vocabulary.

ADDITIONAL MATERIAL

- Customised online modules for specific L1 groups that focus on areas where help is most needed, informed by the Cambridge English Learner Corpus.
- Academic Study Skills online module that prepares students for the challenges of studying a university-level course taught in English.

TAILORED TO SUIT YOUR NEEDS

Mindset for IELTS gives teachers the ultimate flexibility to tailor courses to suit their context and the needs of their students.

GIVES TEACHERS CHOICE

- Course design means teachers can focus on either the skills or the topics that their students need the most help with.

CUSTOMISATION

- Online modules can be used in the classroom as extension work or as extra practice at home, allowing the teacher to customise the length and focus of the course.
- Additional online modules designed for specific L1 learners can be incorporated into the course.

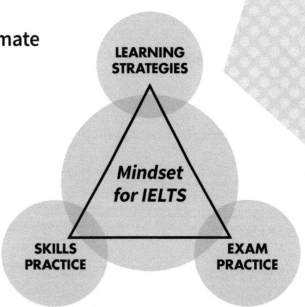

FOUNDATION LEVEL CONFIGURATION

The *Mindset for IELTS* course comprises 5 key components:

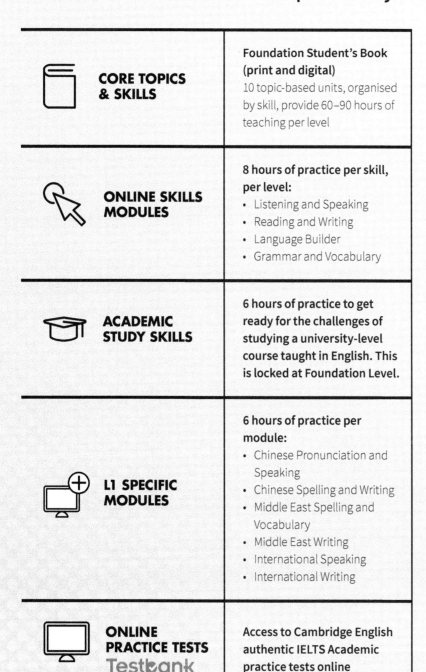

📖	**CORE TOPICS & SKILLS**	Foundation Student's Book (print and digital) 10 topic-based units, organised by skill, provide 60–90 hours of teaching per level
🖱	**ONLINE SKILLS MODULES**	8 hours of practice per skill, per level: • Listening and Speaking • Reading and Writing • Language Builder • Grammar and Vocabulary
🎓	**ACADEMIC STUDY SKILLS**	6 hours of practice to get ready for the challenges of studying a university-level course taught in English. This is locked at Foundation Level.
🖥	**L1 SPECIFIC MODULES**	6 hours of practice per module: • Chinese Pronunciation and Speaking • Chinese Spelling and Writing • Middle East Spelling and Vocabulary • Middle East Writing • International Speaking • International Writing
🖥	**ONLINE PRACTICE TESTS** Testbank	Access to Cambridge English authentic IELTS Academic practice tests online

01▷ SKILLS MODULES

8 hours of practice per module.

- Listening and Speaking
- Reading and Writing

Providing integrated skills to help with development of language and ideas to build confidence with the productive skills

- Language Builder

Providing remedial help and revision of vocabulary and grammar in exam type activities to help with language development

- Grammar and Vocabulary

Providing practice of the grammar and vocabulary that appears in each unit.

02▷ L1 SPECIFIC MODULES

Extra practice for areas that need the most work, informed by the Cambridge Learner Corpus.*

MIDDLE EAST

- Spelling and Vocabulary
- Writing

CHINESE

- Pronunciation and Speaking
- Spelling and Writing

International modules focus on common areas of weakness and are suitable for all first languages.

INTERNATIONAL

- Speaking
- Writing

*Currently the same module is used for Level 1 and Level 2.

UNIT: INTRODUCTION

Student's Book

Mindset for IELTS Foundation Level is aimed at students who are thinking about taking IELTS, but who are currently at an A2 level. It teaches students in a linear way and helps them to improve both their general English level and introduces elements of assessment that are helpful for both the IELTS test and English language assessment in general.It is designed for up to 90 hours classroom use. The topics have been chosen to help students develop their skills and knowledge in connection with everyday topics at the start of the course and introduces topics that will be useful for the IELTS test as they progress.

- Topics have been chosen to suit the needs and abilities of students at this level. They help build confidence at the start of the course whilst stretching them in the later stages, so that they start to get an idea of what they will meet on the IELTS test.
- There is coverage of the type of tasks that students at this level can cope with on the IELTS test and more general activities that will give students the foundation for understanding how assessment items work when they progress to a full IELTS course.
- Each level of *Mindset* is challenging, but doesn't push students above what they can do.

How *Mindset for IELTS Foundation* helps with each skill

In the Foundation level all of the skills are integrated within the unit. This is because students at this level need to be able to see how the skills work with each other. Reading skills help develop the ideas and skills that are needed to complete Writing tasks and Listening skills help to develop the ideas and skills that are needed for the Speaking activities.

- **Speaking –** *Mindset for IELTS Foundation* helps students to develop their skills and confidence on familiar topics that they will need to progress their general English knowledge while also enabling them to become more familiar with the type of questions that they will need to be able to deal with on the IELTS test.
- **Writing –** In the Foundation level students develop their writing skills for everyday communication; become familiar with the type of tasks for Part 1 and Part 2 of the IELTS test; and learn about how these types of writing can be developed and in respect to exam type tasks, how they will be assessed.
- **Reading –** *Mindset for IELTS Foundation* helps develop ideas and language skills that students can use in conjunction with the other skills. It also helps them get used to the types of questions they will face at IELTS in a way that is appropriate for students who are at this level.
- **Listening –** *Mindset for IELTS Foundation* helps to develop strategies for listening and makes students aware of the types of activities that are used on the IELTS test. It also helps to build confidence and develop ideas that will help them with their short-term and long-term linguistic goals.

Outcomes

At the start of every unit you will see a list of outcomes

IN THIS UNIT YOU WILL LEARN HOW TO

- understand activities that people do in their daily routine
- use present simple and adverbs of frequency
- read multiple texts to choose the correct answer
- write describing a daily routine
- read to guess meaning from context
- listen to information about a student exchange trip
- speak about your day

In the Student's Book you will see how these outcomes relate to the unit as a whole and in the Teacher's Book you will see which part of the unit that they refer to. This will help you to decide the best way to develop the skills that your students need. There are typically three or four overarching outcomes that relate to either goals that will help students to progress their overall English ability and knowledge or ones that will give them an insight into the types of skills they will need when they enter a full IELTS course.

Tip Boxes, Bullet Boxes and Mini Tips

- Tip boxes help you and your students improve task awareness and language skills. You will find further information on how to get them most out of them in the Teacher's Book. Note that the number in the corner relates to the exercise that the tip goes with.

TIP 0 6

In this kind of exam task, there is often information about the question in more than one text. Look at the information in green. Think about why B is the correct answer here.

- Bullet boxes tell you how students are assessed in tests and give a better understanding of the task being addressed.

⊙ Try to add more information about your answer and don't give short answers. You can give reasons or examples. Use *because* for reasons and *for example* / *like* for examples.

- Mini tips help with the understanding of discrete questions and items that will help develop an understanding of the type of question being asked. Note that the first number in the corner relates to the exercise number and the second one relates to the question number.

06.1 MINI TIP What is the opposite of the 'same'?

Teacher's Book

The Teacher's Book has been designed to give you a step-by-step look at the activities and how to teach them. It has also been developed in a way that will help you see how the language and skills development relate directly to moving your students in the direction of IELTS.

It also contains the following:

- Extension activities - exercises that give more practice on the skill or area, if you feel that your students need to spend longer on them.
- Alternative activities - ideas that will help you develop ideas to tailor them to your students' needs and/or interests.
- Definitions - to help you with understanding of concepts connected with assessment features that are used both in the IELTS test and other forms of assessment.

There is also a link to all of the classroom audio in the Teacher's Book.

How to use the online modules specific to the Foundation Module

As well as the Student's Book there are also online modules that can aid with further study. These can be used for homework or to reinforce what has been taught in class.

- **Reading and Writing**
- **Speaking and Listening**
- **Language Builder**
- **Grammar and Vocabulary**

The Reading and Writing and Speaking and Listening modules give more practice on the topics that have been studied in the book. They help to develop both ideas and the language skills that the students will need in order to be successful.

The Language Builder builds knowledge of everyday topics and sets them in an IELTS context. It can aid with understanding assessment and to build confidence and knowledge for lower level students.

The Grammar and Vocabulary module presents the grammar and vocabulary from the final section of each unit in a series of interactive exercises

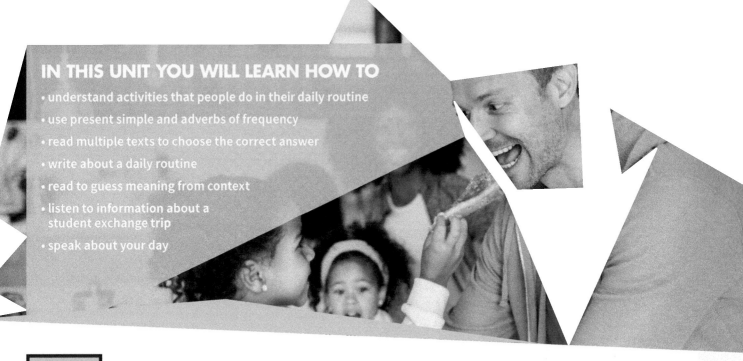

IN THIS UNIT YOU WILL LEARN HOW TO

- understand activities that people do in their daily routine
- use present simple and adverbs of frequency
- read multiple texts to choose the correct answer
- write about a daily routine
- read to guess meaning from context
- listen to information about a student exchange trip
- speak about your day

LEAD-IN

0 1 ► Look at the pictures and read the words. Which of these activities do you do every day? Write five more activities you do every day.

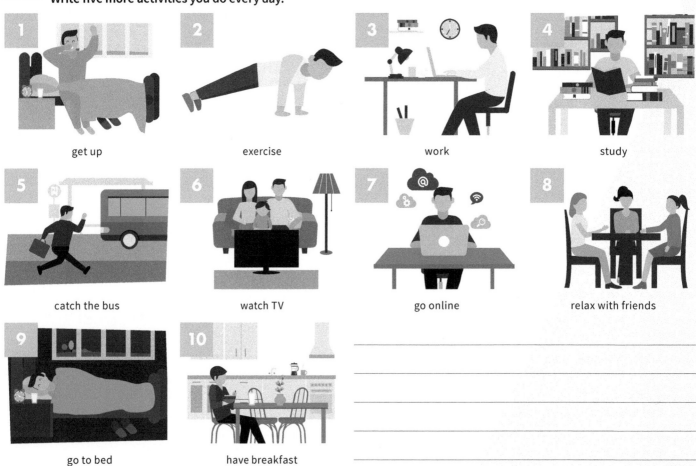

1. get up
2. exercise
3. work
4. study
5. catch the bus
6. watch TV
7. go online
8. relax with friends
9. go to bed
10. have breakfast

0 2 ► In pairs, compare your answers and talk about what time you do each activity.

0 3 Read the sentences about a boy who is doing a language course in the UK. Choose the best answer, A, B or C.

0 Ping _____ at 7:30am every morning and has breakfast with his host family.

Answer: A

   A gets up   **B** stands up   **C** stays up

1 At 8:30am, he _____ the bus to his language school.

   A goes   **B** catches   **C** travels

2 During the day, Ping studies English and _____ to his classmates.

   A laughs   **B** chats   **C** tells

3 Everyone speaks English in his class because the students all _____ from different countries around the world.

   A arrive   **B** live   **C** come

4 After Ping finishes school at 3:00pm, he often _____ some sightseeing in the city with his friends.

   A does   **B** makes   **C** has

5 In the evening, Ping relaxes with his host family, _____ TV or goes online.

   A watches   **B** sees   **C** looks

0 4 In pairs, read and discuss the questions.

1 Do you do any of the activities in Exercise 3?

2 What time does your school, college or job start and finish?

3 What do young people like to do in the evenings in your country?

05▶ You are going to read an article about the daily life of three teenagers from different countries. Skim the text once quickly. Underline the activities that you do in your daily routine.

A DAY IN THE LIFE

Three college students from around the world tell us about their daily routine

AVA AUSTRALIA

I'm from a small town in Queensland. Most people in Australia live near the coast, but we live on a cattle farm in the centre of the country. I get up at around 7am and have breakfast. My mum teaches at my college, so I usually go with her in the car instead of taking the bus. College starts at 8:30am and finishes at 4pm. When I get home, I help my dad on the farm for a few hours. In the evenings, I try to watch TV but I'm usually too tired. I go to bed at about 10:00pm.

NINA NORWAY

I live in a village on Norway's Atlantic coast. I get up at 7:30am and walk to college. Classes begin at 8:30am and finish at 3pm. After that, I go to one of the college clubs. These are not very expensive and there are lots to choose from. I do athletics and football but you can also do things like folk dancing and cross-country skiing. When my parents come home from work, my dad makes dinner and we all eat together. After that, my mum takes me out for a driving lesson. I've got my test soon and I need to practise!

MICHAEL BRAZIL

I live in Rio de Janeiro. I get up at 6am and catch a bus to college at 6:30am. Lessons start at 7:20am. We have a break at 9:50am and then study until 12:30pm. I get home at about 1:40pm. After that, I often go to the beach with my friends to swim in the ocean or play beach volleyball, but I sometimes also just stay at home to sleep or study. In the evenings, I cook dinner for my family, then we watch TV or listen to the radio before bed. I switch off my light at about 10pm.

0 6 Read the article again and the sentences. Choose the best answer, A, B or C.

0 Who finishes studying before 1pm?   **Answer:** __B__
   A Ava   **B** Michael   **C** Nina

1 Who works with a member of the family after college? _____
   A Ava   **B** Michael   **C** Nina

2 Who goes out in the car in the evenings? _____
   A Ava   **B** Michael   **C** Nina

3 Who gets a lift in a car to college most mornings? _____
   A Ava   **B** Michael   **C** Nina

4 Who prepares the evening meal for the family? _____
   A Ava   **B** Michael   **C** Nina

5 Who pays to do extra activities in the afternoons? _____
   A Ava   **B** Michael   **C** Nina

6 Who finds it difficult to watch TV in the evenings? _____
   A Ava   **B** Michael   **C** Nina

7 Who lives a long way from the sea? _____
   A Ava   **B** Michael   **C** Nina

TIP 06

In this kind of exam task, there is often information about the question in more than one text. Look at the information in green. Think about why B is the correct answer here.

06.1 MINI TIP Look at the information in yellow in the article about family members. Which one answers the question correctly?

GRAMMAR AND SPEAKING

0 7 Read the Grammar box. Then, match the questions 1–3 with the answers A–C.

	Group 1	Group 2	Group 3	Group 4
Present simple	Regular verbs	Verbs ending in -s, -ch, -sh, -x	Verbs ending in consonant -y	Verbs ending in -o, -ss, -ch, -sh
I/you/we/they he/she/it …	get up early	watch TV	try hard	go, wash
	gets up early	watches TV	tries hard	goes, washes

Adverbs of frequency

Never	Sometimes	Often	Usually	Always
0%				100%

1 What do we use the present simple for?   **A** -s
2 Why do we use adverbs of frequency?   **B** to talk about every day routines and habits
3 What do verbs for *he/she/it* end in?   **C** to say how often we do something

0 8 In pairs, find examples of the verb groups 1, 2, 3 and 4 in the Lead-in and Reading in Exercise 5.

0 9 Now, you are going to speak about the magazine article in Exercise 5.
Read the task and make notes about what you could say. Then, in pairs, do the task.

- Work in pairs A and B.
- Student A, close your book. Student B, make sentences about Ava, Michael or Nina.
  For example: She has breakfast at 7:00 am. or She goes to clubs after college.
- Student B, can you say who Student A is talking about?
- After 5 minutes, swap roles.

READING: SENTENCE COMPLETION

1 0 ▶ Read the information about the daily routine of a student at a UK university. Complete the text using the verbs in brackets in the correct form.

Dan usually **1** _____ (**get up**) at 8am, **2** _____ (**have**) a shower and **3** _____ (**eat**) breakfast. After that, he always **4** _____ (**get**) his books ready and then **5** _____ (**go**) to his lectures until midday. He usually **6** _____ (**return**) home and **7** _____ (**make**) lunch for himself at about 12:30pm. Then, he sometimes **8** _____ (**watch**) a bit of TV. At about 3pm, he often **9** _____ (**meet**) a friend for coffee. At 3:30pm, they sometimes **10** _____ (**go**) to the library together. Dan always **11** _____ (**study**) for a few hours and then at around 6:30pm he **12** _____ (**go**) home. He usually **13** _____ (**cook**) dinner for himself and his flat mates. In the evening, he sometimes **14** _____ (**exercise**) at the gym or goes for a run. After that, he relaxes in front of the TV or **15** _____ (**see**) his friends. He never goes to bed early, but usually **16** _____ (**fall**) asleep at around midnight.

WRITING: DESCRIBING A DAILY ROUTINE

1 1 ▶ Look again at the information in Exercise 10. Write about your daily routine and the activities you do every day.

I sometimes do the laundry. I never make dinner. My brother often takes out the bins.

TIP 11

Look at the highlighted words in Exercise 10 to see how often Dan does his activities.

READING: MATCHING

1 2 ▶ Read the text and match the phrases that have similar meanings.

I often help a lot around the house and I usually help my mum do the laundry. My brother is lazy and he never washes his clothes. He always leaves them in a pile on his bedroom floor. In the evening after school, I always tidy up my room. I put things away and get my schoolbag ready for the next day. My dad sometimes washes up after dinner. We don't have a dishwasher at the moment because our old one broke down, so he has to clean the dishes by himself. My sister likes cooking, so she often helps mum make lunch and dinner. She prepared a delicious meal of roast chicken at the weekend. Sometimes my brother puts the rubbish out, but he usually just leaves it by the back door instead of taking it out to the bins. We all usually try and help and do the cleaning. When the housework is done, we always relax and watch TV.

1 do the laundry	A take out the bins
2 tidy up	B prepare a meal
3 wash up	C wash the clothes
4 make lunch/dinner	D put things away
5 put the rubbish out	E do the housework
6 do the cleaning	F clean the dishes

1 3 ▷ Look at the following pictures showing Julia Grant, a volunteer on a science project. Using the pictures, write a description of Julia's daily routine. In your description, you should:

- begin like this: *Julia Grant is 21 years old and works as a volunteer on a science project in Fiji. Every morning, she …*
- write what activities she does and what time she does them.
- use sequencing words: *After that … /Next … /Then …*
- use adverbs of frequency.

1 4 ▷ In pairs, compare your texts about Julia Grant. Help each other to correct any mistakes with spelling, grammar or punctuation.

LISTENING: MATCHING

1 5 ▷ Read some information about a website offering student exchange programmes. Decide if the sentences are true T or false F.

Spend a term or a whole year in another country

Stay with a host family and go to a local college. Learn all about the culture, and maybe learn a new language. Make new friends and have a great time. You need to pay for flights and take some pocket money, but that's all. Host families are not paid. All they ask is that you help with jobs around the house and join in with family activities.

Go to *student_exchange.com*
and explore our website to learn more!

15.1 MINI TIP How long does a term normally last at school? It's less than a year.

15.2 MINI TIP What should students bring with them?

15.3 MINI TIP What does 'join in with' mean?

1 All students spend at least a year abroad. T F
2 Host families give students pocket money during their stay. T F
3 Students should do housework and be involved with family activities. T F

16 ▶ You are going to listen to two friends, Carlos and Jack, talking about a student exchange trip. Listen and decide which countries Carlos and Jack come from.

🔊 02

17 ▶ Listen again. What activity does each member of Jack's family like doing? For questions 1–5, write a letter A–H next to each person.

🔊 02

Person		Activity
0 Jack	___H___	**A** cooking
1 Jack's brother	_____	**B** going to the gym
2 Jack's sister	_____	**C** taking care of the garden
3 Jack's mum	_____	**D** doing art
4 Jack's dad	_____	**E** repairing things
5 Jack's grandmother	_____	**F** reading books
		G shopping
		H playing team sports

> **17.0 MINI TIP** Jack says he likes volleyball and basketball, so the answer to this question is 'team sports'. Notice that the answer does not always contain the words you hear, but the meaning is the same.
>
> **17.1 MINI TIP** Be careful! You hear something about the gym, but it isn't the correct answer here.
>
> **17.4 MINI TIP** Pay attention for words with similar meanings. What's a similar word to 'fixing'?

18 ▶ In pairs or small groups, talk about the student exchange trip in Exercise 17 and ask and answer the questions.

1 Would you like to go to another country to study?

2 If no, why not? If yes, which country would you go to?

3 What do you like doing at home? What do your friends and members of your family do?

SPEAKING: TALKING ABOUT YOUR DAY

19 ▶ Read the task. What would you say? Spend two minutes thinking about what you could say and make some notes. In pairs, compare your ideas.

Describe what you usually do on an average day.

You should say:

- what you do.
- who you do it with.
- where you do it.

Explain what you enjoy most about your day and why.

> **TIP 19** You should write only short words or phrases. If you write full sentences, and then read them out, you will lose marks.

> **TIP 19** The first three points are factual. Don't worry if you can't think of anything to say that is true – you can invent something if you need to.

20 ▶ Now, read and do the task.

- Work in pairs.
- Student A: speak for 1–2 minutes about your day.
- Student B: as you listen, write *yes* or *no* beside sentences 1–6.

1 The talk is easy to understand. _____

2 The speaker often pauses and hesitates. _____

3 The speaker stays on the topic of the question. _____

4 The talk is too long. _____

5 The talk is too short. _____

6 The talk is interesting. _____

21 ▶ Swap roles. Student B, you speak for 1–2 minutes about your day and Student A, you listen. Show your feedback to each other and discuss how you can improve.

GRAMMAR AND VOCABULARY

0 1 ▸ **Match the digital times with the times in words.**

1	05:15	A	It's five past ten.
2	08:20	B	It's ten to nine.
3	06:45	C	It's ten past nine.
4	14:30	D	It's twenty past eight.
5	20:50	E	It's quarter to seven.
6	09:10	F	It's twelve o'clock.
7	15:35	G	It's five to five.
8	10:05	H	It's quarter past five.
9	12:00	I	It's twenty-five to four.
10	16:55	J	It's half past two.

0 2 ▸ **Unscramble the letters in brackets to complete the text.**

When I get up in the morning, the first thing that I do is **1** _____ (**avhe**) a shower. I then go to the kitchen and make breakfast. After breakfast, I **2** _____ (**bhusr**) my teeth. Then I **3** _____ (**emte**) my friends and we **4** _____ (**chact**) the bus to the college. At college, we study all day, but we have a break for lunch at 12 o'clock. At four o'clock, we **5** _____ (**vlaee**) the college and **6** _____ (**og**) home by bus. In the evenings, I usually **7** _____ (**cwaht**) TV, unless I have a lot of homework. I always **8** _____ (**od**) my homework in the evenings. At night, I always **9** _____ (**og**) to bed and (**10**)_____ (**lafl**) asleep straight away.

0 3 ▸ **Complete the table using the words in the box.**

a mess	the cleaning	the beds	dinner	some homework
the laundry	a noise	the shopping	the housework	lunch

Make	Do

0 4 Complete the email using the words in the box.

walk	leave	have	finish	get up
catch	go out	work	meet	live

To: Sam
From: Harry

Reply Forward

Hi Sam,

I'm having a great time here in France. I'm learning lots of French. My host family are very nice.

They **1** _____ in an apartment in an area called Pantin, and they both

2 _____ as journalists. They **3** _____ very early in the morning

and **4** _____ the house before me. I **5** _____ breakfast at about

8am and then go to the language school. I usually **6** _____ there, but if I'm late

I **7** _____ the bus. Lessons at the school **8** _____ at 4pm and

we can go home. The other students are very nice and I have made lots of new friends. We

9 _____ after school in a cafe or **10** _____ in the evenings to the cinema.

Harry

0 5 Complete the sentences using the third person form of the verbs in brackets.

1 My dad _____ (**wash**) his car every weekend.
2 Jim _____ (**watch**) too much TV.
3 Adrian's baby _____ (**cry**) a lot.
4 My brother is good at chess and _____ (**practise**) every day.
5 Olga _____ (**go**) jogging most evenings after work.
6 Tom's wife cooks and Tom _____ (**do**) the washing up.
7 Anna _____ (**catch**) the 253 bus to college each morning.
8 Nadia _____ (**relax**) by doing yoga.
9 I think our teacher _____ (**give**) us far too much homework.
10 My brother _____ (**switch off**) his light at about midnight.

0 6 Read the sentences and underline the correct answer.

1 My brother **works** / **work** for a computer company in the city.
2 My friends and I often **play** / **plays** basketball together at the weekends.
3 I go to a college where everyone **study** / **studies** different languages.
4 My grandparents **come** / **comes** from a small village in Germany.
5 In Britain, most school students **wear** / **wears** a uniform.
6 In the evenings, I **like** / **likes** to chat to my friends online.
7 In my family, only my sister **gets up** / **get up** before 6am.
8 I **have** / **has** a dance class every Wednesday evening.
9 My friend is good at baking and **make** / **makes** amazing cakes.
10 My lunch break **begin** / **begins** at 12pm and **finish** / **finishes** at 12:45pm.

07 Reorder the words to make correct sentences.

1 the / my / room / friend / tidies

_____ .

2 play / I / the / football / weekend / at

_____ .

3 a / to / lunch / I / sandwich / for / take / college

_____ .

4 six / past / up / wake / I / at / half

_____ .

5 every / his / my / checks / minutes / brother / phone / five

_____ .

6 in / I / a / have / evening / shower / the

_____ .

7 try / 9pm / to / I / studying / before / stop

_____ .

8 every / go / to / months / I / the / dentist / six

_____ .

9 my / the / housework / of / does / father / most

_____ .

10 visit / at / I / my / the / family / weekends

_____ .

08 Complete the email using the words in the box.

shouts   work   opens   work   enjoy   start
fill   clean   take   tidy   tells   finish   gets

Reply Forward ✉

To: Hannah

From: William

I have got a new job! It's in a supermarket and I **1** _____ there every
Saturday. I **2** _____ at 8am and the shop **3** _____
at 9am. I **4** _____ the shelves with food products and
5 _____ the shopping baskets by the entrance.
I **6** _____ the floors and **7** _____ at the checkout.
My manager is very nice. She **8** _____ me what to do and never
9 _____ . The other workers are really friendly, too. We
10 _____ three breaks a day and **11** _____ at 4pm.
It's hard work because the shop **12** _____ very busy, but I really
13 _____ it.

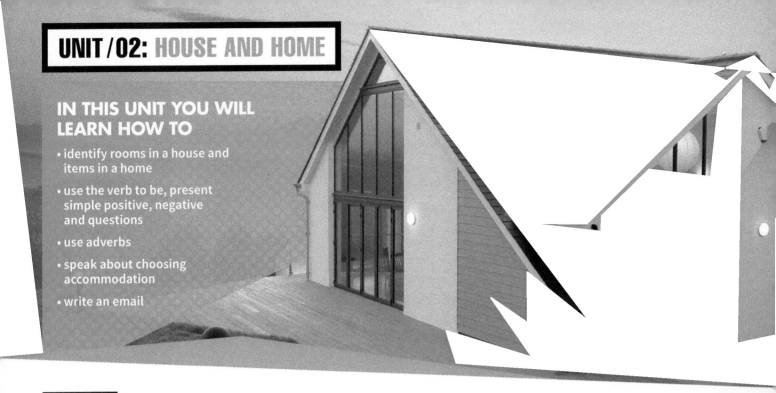

UNIT / 02: HOUSE AND HOME

IN THIS UNIT YOU WILL LEARN HOW TO

- identify rooms in a house and items in a home
- use the verb to be, present simple positive, negative and questions
- use adverbs
- speak about choosing accommodation
- write an email

01▷ Look at the pictures of rooms in a house. What rooms are they? Complete the words with the missing letters.

b _ _ _ _ _ _ _

b _ _ _ _ _ _ _

k _ _ _ _ _ _ _

l _ _ _ _ _ _
r _ _ _

02▷ Look at some other places that you find in and around a house. Then, match the names in the box to the pictures.

| garden   hall   hallway   basement   attic   garage   study |

   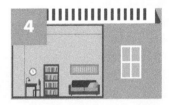

_____   _____   _____   _____

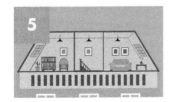 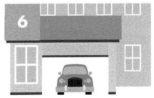 

_____   _____   _____

03▶ In pairs, you are going to talk together about some pictures. Read and do the task.

- **Student A**, look at the pictures – do you know what they show?
- **Student B**, tell Student A if their answers are correct.

1

2

3

4

5

6

- **Student B**, look at the pictures – do you know what they show?
- **Student A**, tell Student B if their answers are correct.

1

2

3

4

5

6

04▶ Now, label the items in Exercise 3.

05▶ What other items can you find in a home? In pairs, make a list of the items.

SPEAKING AND VOCABULARY

06 ▶ In pairs, discuss the differences between the items or places. You can use a dictionary to help you.

1 A house and an apartment / flat.
2 Curtains and blinds.
3 A fridge and a freezer.
4 A study and a living room.
5 A bath and a sink.

LISTENING 1: PICTURE DESCRIPTION

07 ▶ You are going to listen to a student, Giorgio, describing his bedroom. Listen and decide which picture is Giorgio's bedroom.

03

TIP 07

During the exam, listen carefully to all the information before choosing your answer.

08 ▶ Now, cover the pictures in Exercise 7 with a piece of paper and listen again. Then, answer the question using TWO or THREE words.

03

1 How does Giorgio describe his bed? _____

2 What can he see outside of his window? _____

3 Why does he play games on his phone? _____

4 Where is the bathroom? _____

5 What does he always do before he goes to college every morning?

_____

6 What is at the window? _____

In tests and exams, you may be asked to write one, two or three words. Do not write more or less than you are asked to write.

09 ▷ In Listening 1, Giorgio spoke about going to university. Before he goes, he needs to organise his accommodation. He emails his friend Gavin for help and advice. Read the advert and the email. Then, complete Giorgio's notes.

TIP 09

Make sure you compare the information in the email to what you can see in the advert.

Prime Location Agency

We find accommodation for university students coming to the UK.

Taylor

Andrew Taylor

We are based in our office in London, but we have flats and rooms in locations all over the country.

📞 020 7219 4386

✉️ andrewtaylor@uniaccom.com

To: Giorgio
From: Gavin

Reply Forward

Hi Giorgio,

Here is the information you need. Mr Taylor is the best agent in the UK for helping you with your future accommodation. He can definitely find you somewhere nice to live. He only works in the office from Monday to Saturday, but you can contact him any time you want by email. Oh, one more thing – the advert has a mistake. His email address finishes with *.co.uk* and not *.com*.

Gavin

Giorgio's notes:

Name of person to contact: **1** _____

Name of Company: **2** _____

Office location: **3** _____

Email: **4** _____

Contact: Monday to Saturday – in the office. Sunday – **5** _____

1 0 ▶ Look at the table and read the questions and statements. Giorgio decides to make a phone call to Andrew Taylor. What might they ask or say to each other? Put a tick ✓ next to the question or statement each one might ask or say.

	Giorgio	Andrew Taylor
1 **Are you** a student?		
2 I **am** a student.		
3 What do **you want** to study?		
4 I **live** with my parents at the moment.		
5 **Can you speak** English?		
6 **Where is** the accommodation?		

GRAMMAR: SIMPLE PRESENT POSITIVE, NEGATIVE AND QUESTIONS

1 1 ▶ Look at the words in bold in the table in Exercise 10. Then, complete the positive '+' and negative '–' statements and questions '?' in the chart.

	Statements and *Yes/No* questions with the verb *to be*	Statements and *Yes/No* questions with other verbs	Statements and *Yes/No* questions with *can*	Questions with question words + the verb *to be* OR other verbs
Positive (+)	I am a student.	I 2 _____ with my parents.	I 5 _____ speak English very well.	
Negative (–)	I 1 _____ a student.	I do not/don't live with my parents. He/She 3 _____ with his/her parents.	I can not/cannot/can't speak English very well.	
Questions (?)	Are you a student?	Do you live with your parents? 4 _____ he/she live with his/her parents?	6 _____ he/she _____ English?	Where is the accommodation? What do 7_____ to study? Why 8 _____ he/she want to live in the UK?

1 2 ▶ Complete the sentences using the correct words.

The car _____ is _____ in the garage. (+)
1 The car _____ in the garage. (–)
2 _____ in the garage? (?)
3 Where _____ the car? (?)
I play games on my phone in my bedroom.
4 _____ games on my phone in my bedroom. (–)
5 _____ games on your phone in your bedroom? (?)
6 What games _____ on your phone? (?)
7 Can _____ a game on my phone later? (?)

LISTENING 2: SHORT ANSWERS

13▷ Listen to a conversation between Giorgio and Andrew Taylor who works at the accommodation agency. What do they discuss? Circle YES or NO.

1	The course Giorgio wants to study at university.	YES	NO
2	His study habits.	YES	NO
3	The number of other students that also live there.	YES	NO
4	Two types of accommodation.	YES	NO
5	The teachers and lecturers at the university.	YES	NO
6	Where the accommodation is.	YES	NO
7	Giorgio's travel options from home to university.	YES	NO
8	The different types of food you can eat there.	YES	NO

13.1 MINI TIP Do you hear the exact name of a course?

13.2 MINI TIP How many options for accommodation does Andrew Taylor give?

13.3 MINI TIP Does Andrew Taylor mention a number?

READING: DIALOGUE BUILDING AND MATCHING

14▷ Read the sentences from Giorgio and Andrew Taylor's conversation and choose the best answer, A, B or C.

1 Good afternoon, Prime Location Agency, Andrew Taylor speaking. _____
2 Oh, hello, Giorgio. Thank you for your call, I have some questions for you. _____
3 First of all, _____ – in a room on campus or in private accommodation?
4 I'm not sure. _____
5 Well, tell me a little about your personality and your preferences. _____
6 OK, that's great. _____ sometimes have a quiet room to study in private?
7 If you live in private accommodation, you have a quiet life with maybe one or two other students who are your housemates. Although, it often takes a long time to travel to university. _____
8 OK, one final question. Would you prefer to live somewhere which is catered? I'm not sure. _____

1 A Can I check your student status?
  B Can I give you my student status?
  C Have you got time to speak? Can you check my student status?

2 A I hope that you don't mind.
  B I hope that you mind.
  C Do you mind?

3 A Where you want to live?
  B Where you do want to live?
  C Where do you want to live?

4 A You can give me some advice?
  B Can you give me some advice?
  C Can give me you some advice?

5 A Are you a sociable person?
  B You are a sociable person?
  C Do you be a sociable person?

6 A Do you also like to
  B You also like to
  C Do you also like

7 A What you think?
  B What you do think?
  C What do you think?

8 A What is *catered* mean?
  B What does *catered* mean?
  C What means *catered*?

15▷ Listen again to the conversation in Exercise 13 and check your answers.

16 ▶ Read the rest of the conversation between Giorgio and Andrew Taylor. Complete the conversation with the correct sentences A–H. There is one example.

 Sometimes in tests, there are more answers than questions, so be careful to make sure you choose the best option.

Andrew: Do you have another question you want to ask me?

Giorgio: 1 __D__

Andrew: I think the house has superfast broadband. The Wi-Fi is sometimes very busy and slow on campus.

Giorgio: 2 _____

Andrew: You also have a TV in the private room, so you can connect your computer and **play** games on the TV.

Giorgio: 3 _____

Andrew: No, but you or your roommate can bring one.

Giorgio: 4 _____

Andrew: Yes, it's good because you can study together.

Giorgio: 5 _____

Andrew: Would you like to discuss everything with your parents?

Giorgio: 6 _____

Andrew: OK. Let me email you some information. You can contact me again after you read it.

A Oh, great. Do the rooms on campus also have TVs?

B Really? I like the idea of having a roommate.

C It's important to me to have a shower in the room.

D Yes. Is the Wi-Fi connection better on campus or in the private house?

E Yes, but I prefer to study alone. Oh, I don't know what to choose.

F Yes, that's a good idea. They always give me good advice.

G Oh, that's good to know. I really like playing online games, you see.

H My room in my parents' house is on the second floor.

READING AND GRAMMAR

17 ▶ Now, think about what you do each morning. In pairs, ask and answer the questions.

1 On a weekday morning, what time does your alarm go off?

2 What time do you get up during the week?

3 Do you like to have a lie in at the weekend? If you do, what time do you get up?

18▷ Read how Giorgio describes what he does before and after he goes to university each day. For each question, choose the best answer A, B or C.

Every weekday morning, my alarm goes **1** _____ at 8:30am. This gives me enough time to get ready before my lectures start at 10:00am. Then, I **2** _____ up and go downstairs. I'm often too tired to eat breakfast, so I sometimes go to the **3** _____ and just get some juice. I always talk to my housemates if they are there, in the **4** _____ . After that, I head back upstairs to get ready. I go to the bathroom, **5** _____ my teeth, and sometimes **6** _____ my room. When it's time to leave, I pack my bag and go to college. At the end of the day when I get back home, I sometimes help the others with the **7** _____ – if we don't do it, all the rooms we share get very messy. When the house is clean again, we usually spend some time in the living room. We sit down together on the **8** _____ and play games online for a while. We're always happy when we get the chance to do this, as it helps us relax. Before I go to sleep, I sit at my **9** _____ and do my homework. I never forget to do it. At the weekend, I can finally relax. I have a lie **10** _____ until about 11:30am.

1	A up	B on	C off
2	A get	B go	C put
3	A fridge	B sink	C freezer
4	A basement	B kitchen	C bathroom
5	A wash	B tidy	C brush
6	A wash	B tidy	C brush
7	A homework	B housework	C workhouse
8	A chair	B desk	C sofa
9	A desk	B bed	C drawers
10	A on	B up	C in

19▷ Look again at what Giorgio says in Exercise 18. Then, underline all the adverbs of frequency.

Example: I am <u>often</u> too tired to eat breakfast.

20▷ Now, put a circle around the main verb next to the adverb.

Example: I (am) <u>often</u> too tired to eat breakfast

21▷ Complete the table using *before* or *after*.

When I use the verb *to be* …	When I use other verbs …
The <u>adverb</u> comes **1** _____ the verb.	The <u>adverb</u> comes **2** _____ the verb.
For example: I am <u>often</u> too tired to eat breakfast.	For example: We <u>usually</u> spend time in the living room in the evenings … .

22▷ Complete the sentences with the adverb *never* in the correct position.

1 I _____ am _____ late for school.
2 I _____ forget _____ to do my homework.

23▷ In pairs, speak about what you usually do on weekdays and describe a typical day for you at the weekend.

2 4 ▶ Look at the information in the boxes that Andrew Taylor gave to Giorgio.
In pairs, answer and discuss the question.

1 Which accommodation is best for Giorgio?

CAMPUS ACCOMMODATION

- Five minutes walk to lecture hall (always)
- Fast Wi-Fi connection (sometimes slow at busy times)
- All bedrooms on floors 2, 3 and 4
- Single bed – no pillows or sheets provided
- Shared bathroom on every floor
- Modern apartment block (160 bedrooms in total)
- Live with 159 other students
- All meals included

PRIVATE ACCOMMODATION

- 25 minute bus ride to lecture hall (usually – sometimes longer)
- Superfast Wi-Fi (always)
- Bedroom on ground floor
- Double bed – pillows and sheets provided
- Private bathroom
- Detached house (three bedrooms in total)
- Live with two other students and the homeowner
- No meals included

2 5 ▶ Which accommodation in Exercise 24 would you prefer? Use the questions below to help you decide.

1 In your opinion, what is more important, having superfast Wi-Fi speed or having a short walk to lectures?

2 Do you prefer the idea of having a pillow and sheets provided or not? Why?

3 How do you like the idea of a room on the ground floor?

4 Are you unhappy about the idea of sharing a bathroom with other students? Or does it not matter to you?

5 What do you think about having all your meals included?

6 What are the advantages of living with lots of other students? And what are the disadvantages?

WRITING: AN EMAIL TO A FRIEND ABOUT ACCOMMODATION

2 6 ▷ Read the email Giorgio received from his friend Gavin. Choose the best answer, A, B or C.

The main reason for writing is:

A to say thank you to Giorgio.
B to ask Giorgio for advice.
C to tell Giorgio that he likes university.

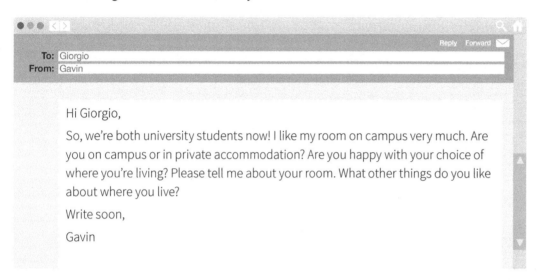

To: Giorgio
From: Gavin

Hi Giorgio,

So, we're both university students now! I like my room on campus very much. Are you on campus or in private accommodation? Are you happy with your choice of where you're living? Please tell me about your room. What other things do you like about where you live?

Write soon,

Gavin

2 7 ▷ Look at Giorgio's reply. He does not use correct punctuation or capital letters. Re-write the email and correct the mistakes.

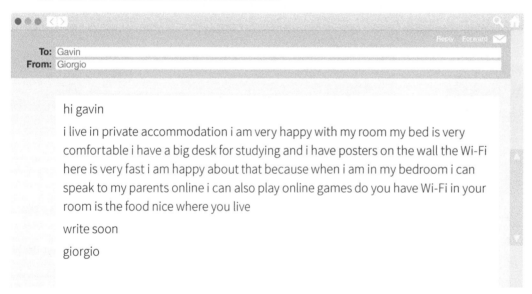

To: Gavin
From: Giorgio

hi gavin

i live in private accommodation i am very happy with my room my bed is very comfortable i have a big desk for studying and i have posters on the wall the Wi-Fi here is very fast i am happy about that because when i am in my bedroom i can speak to my parents online i can also play online games do you have Wi-Fi in your room is the food nice where you live

write soon

giorgio

2 8 ▷ Imagine you are Gavin. Reply to Giorgio and answer his questions. Then ask him two questions about his accommodation. Write 60–80 words.

GRAMMAR AND VOCABULARY

01▶ Read the definitions of places in and around the home and write the correct words.

1 This is the place where you usually sleep every night. _____

2 This is the place where you have a wash and brush your teeth. _____

3 This is the place where people usually sit together to talk, play games or watch TV.
_____

4 This is the place where you keep the car. _____

5 This is the place that you walk through to move from one room to another.
_____

6 This is the place where you can be outside and sit on the grass. _____

02▶ Look at the pictures and underline the correct answer.

a fridge / a freezer

a terraced house /
a semi-detached house

a desk / some drawers

a living room / a study

an attic / a basement

a wardrobe / a cupboard

a chair / a sofa

a university campus /
a private apartment block

0 3 ▷ Match the questions and answers.

1 What do you like about your room?
2 Who do you live with?
3 Do you like to cook?
4 Where do you watch television?
5 Is it often sunny where you live?
6 Where do you do your homework?
7 Can you tell me where the bathroom is, please?
8 Why don't you often go in the kitchen?

A Usually in the living room and sometimes in my bedroom.
B Usually in the study and sometimes in my bedroom.
C My comfortable bed and my posters.
D Yes. Go down the hall and it is next to the living room.
E My parents, my sister and my grandparents.
F Because I can't cook!
G Yes, and I think I'm quite good at it.
H Yes. I like it because I can spend time in the garden.

0 4 ▷ Find the 11 words about places and things in and around a home.

E	Y	D	B	S	H	O	W	E	R
K	P	G	A	R	D	E	N	M	S
O	B	B	S	T	U	D	Y	W	I
K	V	W	E	R	K	G	T	E	N
I	V	S	M	S	B	M	N	E	K
T	E	L	E	V	I	S	I	O	N
C	N	D	N	X	Z	R	V	S	N
H	I	L	T	A	T	T	I	C	F
E	S	Q	W	I	N	D	O	W	K
N	X	J	P	M	B	L	I	N	D

0 5 ▷ Correct the spelling mistake in orange in each sentence.

1 I really like my certains – they are red and black, and they make my bedroom very dark. _____

2 I have a bright tabel lamb that I use when I do my homework. _____

3 I think potsers make the walls look more interesting – don't you? _____

4 It is good to sleep with two bilows – it is very comfortable. _____

5 My brother never cooks – the only thing he can do is turn on the uven!

_____

6 Most of my clothes are in my walldrobe – the rest are in the drawers next to my bed. _____

06▷ **Rewrite the sentences using the question form.**

0 You help your parents with the housework.
Do you help your parents with the housework?

1 It is okay to come to your house this evening.

_____

2 You can check that the windows are all closed before we go out.

_____

3 You are in the living room next to the kitchen.

_____

4 You want to sit in the garden.

_____

5 The apartments in the UK are very different from the apartments in your country.

_____

07▷ **Find and underline the mistakes. Rewrite the mistake correctly. Some sentences are correct.**

1 In my country, people live usually in apartments and not houses. _____

2 My uncle keeps his car always in the garage because it is very expensive. _____

3 Our sink sometimes makes a very strange noise. _____

4 I have a housemate but I don't see very often him – he is always studying. _____

5 In your country, do people usually celebrate their 18th birthday with a party? _____

6 Do you prefer to do your homework in your bedroom? _____

08▷ **Reorder the words to make correct sentences.**

1 does / he / washing / never / up / the

_____

2 me / advice / you / some / give / can / ?

_____

3 eight / house / leave / morning / the / I / in / always / at / my / o'clock

_____

4 off / time / your / does / what / alarm / go / usually / ?

_____

5 often / dinner / house / my / comes / to / cousin / for / my

_____

6 live / future / do / the / where / to / in / want / you / ?

_____

7 live / how / you / do / with / people / many / ?

_____

8 on / campus / live / you / do / university / the

_____

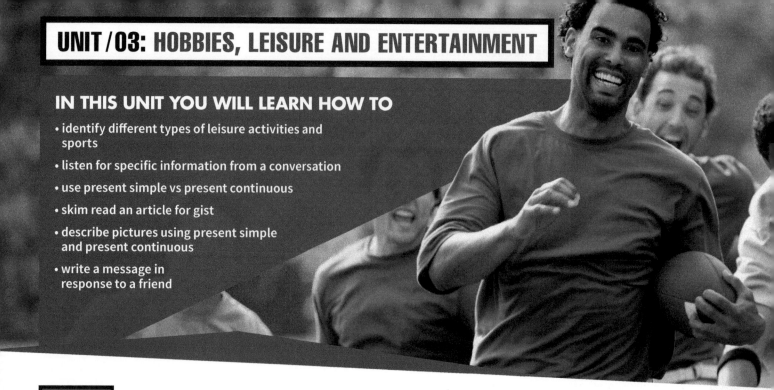

UNIT /03: HOBBIES, LEISURE AND ENTERTAINMENT

IN THIS UNIT YOU WILL LEARN HOW TO

- identify different types of leisure activities and sports
- listen for specific information from a conversation
- use present simple vs present continuous
- skim read an article for gist
- describe pictures using present simple and present continuous
- write a message in response to a friend

01▶ Match the leisure activities in the box to the pictures. There are three extra activities you do not need to use.

cycling	white water rafting	shopping	sailing
climbing	cooking	hiking	canoeing	reading

What do you think about the activities in Exercise 1? Complete the table using the activities from the word box in Exercise 1 that are true for you. Add three more activities to each group.

fun	scary	boring

In pairs, compare your ideas. Then, discuss the questions.

1 Have you ever done any of these activities in Exercise 1?

2 What activities do you do in your free time? What activities do you like to do on holiday?

3 What activities are popular in your country?

LISTENING: MULTIPLE CHOICE QUESTIONS

 Listen to two friends, Deon and Mark, talking about an adventure holiday. Which activities from Exercise 1 do you hear?

 Listen again and choose the correct answer, A, B or C.

0 When will Deon and Mark go on the adventure holiday?

A June

B July

C August

Answer: C

1 How did Deon first find out about *World Trek* holidays?

A He has been on one of their holidays.

B He found their website online.

C He heard about it from someone he knows.

2 Deon would like to go on an adventure holiday

A in a forest.

B in the mountains.

C near the sea.

3 How much does the holiday they want to go on cost if they book it now?

A £500

B £650

C £800

4 The price of the holiday does NOT include

A food.

B the guide.

C transport.

5 What time will the boys meet this evening?

A 7pm

B 7:30 pm

C 8pm

 In Listening exams, you will hear information about all three answer options but only one will be the correct answer.

 In some Listening exam exercises, the words in the answer options will be different from the words you hear.

05.0 MINI TIP Mark says he can't go on holiday in June or July because he has college.

05.1 MINI TIP Deon says, 'a friend told me', which matches the answer option 'someone he knows'. Listen for the meaning, not just the same words. You can see another example of this in question 4.

GRAMMAR: PRESENT SIMPLE / PRESENT CONTINUOUS

06▷ Read the blog entry and look at the verbs in purple. Then, complete the table using the verbs from the blog entry. There are two examples.

MY BLOG

ABOUT   POSTS   COMMENTS

SUNDAY   12:46pm   13 likes

I'm having a great time here in Iceland. I don't miss home at all.
I'm not staying in a hotel. I'm staying at a little guesthouse with 11 other people.
Every day, we get up early and go hiking or climbing. At the moment, I'm resting in my room because I'm exhausted. At home, I usually sleep about eight hours a night but on this holiday I need at least 10 hours a night because I'm so active!

Our guide is great. He looks after us really well and he always makes us laugh.
I'm happy with the food, but my friend doesn't like it very much. Today, we're having reindeer burgers. The chef is cooking them now and they smell delicious.

HERE ARE A FEW PHOTOS OF MY TRIP SO FAR.

In this picture, we're riding Icelandic ponies.

This is my group. They're hiking near a beautiful waterfall.

My friend is climbing a volcano. It's really hard work!

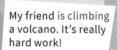

Present simple		Present continuous	
affirmative	**negative**	**affirmative**	**negative**
We get up			I'm not staying

07▷ Look again at the verbs in Exercise 6. Then, complete the grammar rules with *simple* or *continuous*.

1 We use the present _____ with time words and phrases, such as *at the moment*, *today* and *now*.

2 We use the present _____ with adverbs, such as *always*, *sometimes*, *usually* and *every day*.

3 We use the present _____ to talk about habits and routines.

4 We use the present _____ to describe the action in photographs.

08▶ **Rewrite the verbs using the third person -s / -es / -ies and the -ing form.**

1 live _____ _____
2 get _____ _____
3 carry _____ _____
4 hope _____ _____
5 wash _____ _____
6 run _____ _____
7 play _____ _____

8 ride _____ _____
9 lie _____ _____
10 pass _____ _____
11 cry _____ _____
12 make _____ _____
13 see _____ _____
14 begin _____ _____

09▶ **Match the questions 1–4 with the answers A–D. Then, complete the grammar rules with *simple* or *continuous*.**

1 Are you enjoying your holiday?
2 What are you doing at the moment?
3 Do you usually get up early?
4 When does your brother get up?

A Yes, I do./No, I don't.
B At about 7am.
C Yes, I am. / No, I'm not.
D I'm having a rest.

5 When you make a question in the present _____ , use the auxiliary verb *do*.
6 When you make a question in the present _____ , use the question form of the verb *to be*.

10▶ **Read the conversations. Then, complete the sentences using the verbs in brackets in the correct form.**

⊙ In exams, you will need to show that you have an understanding of different verb tenses and how to use them in sentences, conversations and longer texts.

1 A Hi, Gabby. What _____ (you/do) at the moment? Do _____ (want) to go out somewhere?
   B I can't, sorry. I _____ (watch) a football match on TV. My team usually _____ (play) really well but they _____ (lose) very badly today!
   A Oh, no! Maybe another time then.

2 A Tom, I _____ (wait) for you outside the cinema. Where are you?
   B I'm sorry, I'm still on the bus. It's terrible – this bus never _____ (arrive) on time.
   A Oh, OK. See you soon.

3 A Hi, Jane. Sam _____ (not answer) my calls today. Is there something the matter with him?
   B No, he's fine. It's just that he's got a French exam next week, so he _____ (study) at the moment.

4 A How _____ usually _____ (you/get) to college Chris?
   B I _____ (walk). It _____ (not take) long. What about you?
   A My Dad usually _____ (drive) me there but he _____ (work) today.
   B Well, let's walk together.

11 ▶ Now, write questions using the words in the present simple or present continuous forms. Then, in pairs, ask and answer the questions.

1 Why / learn / English?

_____

2 What time / usually / get up?

_____

3 What / learn about / in geography at the moment?

_____

4 play / tennis?

_____

5 What / teacher / do / now?

_____

READING: USE OF DISTRACTION

12 ▶ You are going to read an article about a sportsperson. First, look at the photos and skim read the article once quickly. Then, in pairs, answer the questions.

1 Who do you think Aimee Fuller is?
2 What sport has Aimee become successful in?
3 What is the reason for this article?

AIMEE FULLER
SNOWBOARDING STAR

Aimee Fuller was born in England but now lives in the USA. She moved to the east coast of the United States at the age of 12 because she knew she wanted to be a professional snowboarder. It wasn't possible to train properly in her hometown because it hardly ever snowed. There was a dry ski slope in her town, where she learnt how to ski and snowboard, but there weren't any mountains with snow to practise the sport.

Aimee quickly found sponsors and a coach when she arrived in the USA, and she is now a successful and well-known snowboarding star. She has done really well in many national competitions and her dream is to win an Olympic gold medal one day.

Aimee spends most of her time practising on the snow, and trains in the gym four to five times a week. She also goes cycling and running. Aimee says it is very important to keep fit because that helps her stay safe when she is doing snowboarding tricks and jumps. Her advice to people who want to learn how to do jumps, is to start small and only do bigger jumps when they feel ready.

DURING HER FREE TIME, AIMEE LIKES TO SPEND TIME AT HOME, SWITCH OFF HER PHONE AND LAPTOP AND HANG OUT WITH HER FRIENDS AND FAMILY.

13▶ Read the article in Exercise 12 again and choose the correct answer, A, B or C.

Ex: Aimee spent the first few years of her life in England.

A True   B False   C Not Given

Answer: A

1 Aimee learnt to ski before she started snowboarding.

   A True   B False   C Not Given

2 It often snowed during winter in Aimee's hometown.

   A True   B False   C Not Given

3 It took Aimee a long time to find a coach after she moved to the USA.

   A True   B False   C Not Given

4 Aimee has won an Olympic medal.

   A True   B False   C Not Given

5 Aimee practises snowboarding in the mountains at least three times a week.

   A True   B False   C Not Given

6 Aimee thinks that snowboarding is more dangerous for her when she is not fit.

   A True   B False   C Not Given

7 In her free time, Aimee prefers being with people to spending time on her laptop.

   A True   B False   C Not Given

14▶ Complete the words from the article to match the descriptions.

1 This is someone who is paid to do a sport or other activity. _ _ _ _ _ _ _ _ _ _ _ _

2 This means to practise your sport. _ _ _ _ _

3 This word describes someone who is doing well in his/her life. _ _ _ _ _ _ _ _ _ _

4 When you are this, you don't get tired easily when you exercise or do sport. _ _ _

5 You ask someone for this when you want to know what to do. _ _ _ _ _ _

SPEAKING AND VOCABULARY

15▶ Look at the picures. Then, in pairs, answer the questions.

In which of these activities do you

1 catch a ball?

2 throw a ball?

3 kick a ball?

4 hit a ball?

5 score a goal?

6 win or lose a match or competition?

7 get fit?

8 use a racket?

9 move a piece?

10 relax your mind?

11 play in a team?

12 play alone?

13 need to wear special clothes?

_____

_____

_____

_____

_____

_____

16▶ In pairs, add more activities that you know to Exercise 15. Which pair in your class can think of the most?

17▶ In the same pairs, look at the pictures in Exercise 15 again and describe what is happening in each one.

18▷ Now, in your pairs, you are going to talk about a different sport. First, decide what sport you are going to talk about. Then, follow the task.

- Student A, describe your sport.
- Student B, you must guess what the sport is. Ask questions to find out more information. You can use the questions in Exercise 15.
- Student A, answer yes or no, but do not say what the sport is.
- Ask and answer questions until Student B guesses correctly. Then, swap roles.

A: *In this sport, you have to hit a ball over a net.*

B: *Do you use a racket?*

A: *Yes.*

B: *Is it tennis?*

A: *Yes!*

19▷ Work in different pairs. You are going to describe a picture. Read the instructions and do the task.

- Student A, look at picture 1.
- Student B, look at picture 2.
- Take turns to say what is happening in your picture.
- Find five things that are the same in the two pictures, and five differences between them.

20▷ In small groups, talk about your hobbies and interests. Ask and answer the questions.

1 What activities do you like doing in your free time?
2 Which sports do you like doing? Which sports do you watch on TV?
3 Is it important to spend time outdoors? Why/Why not?

2 1 ▶ Read some information about a film festival and an email you received from your friend, Andrew. Then, complete the notes.

Reply Forward ✉

To: Joshua
From: Andrew

Hi Joshua,

I'm emailing you about the film festival at the weekend.
I can only go on Saturday as I'm working on Sunday.
I don't mind if we miss *Blue Rain*, but I can't wait to see
Child in Time! We can get food there, but don't forget an
umbrella as it looks like the weather won't be good.

I'll get the tickets online tonight and you can pay me then.

See you at the entrance at 1:00pm.

Andrew

Film festival with Andrew

Place: **(0)** _____Sunnyhill Park_____

Date we will go: **1** _____

Cost for me: **2** £_____

Time to meet Andrew: **3** _____

Film we will see: **4** _____

What to take: **5** _____

FILM FESTIVAL IN SUNNYHILL PARK

SATURDAY 23RD AND SUNDAY 24TH JUNE

2:00PM *Blue Rain*

4:00PM *Child in Time*

TICKETS: £20 on the day or £15 from
www.parkcinema.com

Also available – food stalls, art and other activities

2|2▶ You and Andrew are now at the film festival. You receive a message on your phone from another friend, Richard. Read the message. What does Richard want to do?

> Hi Joshua,
>
> Where are you? Are you busy? I'm watching TV at home at the moment but I'm really bored.
>
> Do you want to meet up? Let me know soon!
>
> Richard

2|3▶ Use the information from this unit to write a message in reply to Richard in Exercise 22. In your message, you should include:

- where you are
- who you are with
- what you are doing
- what is happening
- where you can meet Richard
- what Richard should bring

2|4▶ In pairs, compare your answers. Check your answers for mistakes with spelling and punctuation, and make sure you have used present tenses correctly.

MODEL ANSWER

Hi Richard,

Yes, that would be great! I'm in Sunnyhill Park at the moment, at a film festival, with Andrew.

We're watching *Child in Time* now – it's fantastic! You can walk around and see any film you like. Send me a message if you can come and I'll meet you at the entrance when you arrive.

Bring some money for food and an umbrella as it may rain.

See you soon,

Joshua

01▶ Match the different activities in the box to the pictures.

| badminton | skiing | football | sailing | swimming | volleyball | hiking | tennis | basketball | cycling |

02▶ Complete the table using the words in the box.

tennis	taekwondo	gymnastics	chess	volleyball	horse-riding	basketball
table tennis	athletics	badminton	karate	skiing	judo	cycling	sailing
hiking	football	hockey	canoeing	bowling	swimming	fishing	boxing

play	do	go

03▶ Complete the sentences using the verbs in the correct form in the box.

| score | win | kick | play | hit | throw | catch | lose | beat |

1 I'm playing in a tennis tournament tomorrow. I hope I _____ some of my matches.
2 Our school football team is not doing well this term. Every team we play against _____ us.
3 I really want to learn how to _____ baseball but it isn't a popular sport in Britain.
4 It is quite difficult to learn how to _____ the ball with the racket when you start playing tennis.
5 When you _____ a sports match, it is important to learn from your mistakes and do better next time.
6 In rugby, players usually pass the ball to each other by _____ it.
7 In football, players can't hold the ball – they must move it by _____ it.
8 In baseball, players wear a special glove on their hand to help them _____ the ball.
9 In football and handball, the team that _____ the most goals is the winner.

04▶ Read the sentences about the sport cricket and underline the correct answer.

1 Cricket is a **popular** / **good** / **favourite** sport in several countries around the world, including India and Britain.
2 There are 11 people in a cricket **team** / **group** / **set**.
3 You play the sport by **throwing** / **hitting** / **kicking** a hard red ball with a bat.
4 It can take five days to compete a cricket **goal** / **match** / **point**.
5 People often **use** / **wear** / **put** white clothes to play cricket.

05▶ Find the odd word out in each set. Then, complete the reason why it is the odd one out using the words in the box.

| team sports | actions used in sports | sports equipment |
| types of competition | water sports | mountain sports |

1 sailing   swimming   tennis   canoeing   windsurfing   _____
The others are _____ .

2 football   rugby   cricket   athletics   baseball   _____
The others are _____ .

3 catch   hit   kick   lose   run   _____
The others are _____ .

4 match   game   tournament   race   judo   _____
The others are _____ .

5 snowboarding   boxing   skiing   climbing   hiking   _____
The others are _____ .

6 ball   winner   bat   racket   stick   _____
The others are _____ .

06▶ Complete the table using the third person present simple form and the -ing form of the verbs.

	third person present simple	-ing form
1 snow		
2 fix		
3 get		
4 stop		
5 invite		
6 marry		
7 wash		
8 make		
9 offer		
10 buy		
11 cross		
12 copy		
13 dance		
14 swim		
15 happen		
16 travel		

07▶ Match the sentence halves.

1 My mum is working _____   A like doing in his free time?
2 I often go to the cinema _____   B in Italy at the moment.
3 I can't speak to you right now _____   C at the weekend?
4 What does your brother _____   D because I'm studying.
5 In this photo, I'm climbing _____   E eating his sandwich?
6 What do you usually do _____   F on a Saturday evening.
7 Why isn't Sam _____   G a volcano with my uncle.

08▷ Read the sentences and underline the correct answer.

1 **I don't know** / I'm not knowing how to play tennis, but I would like to learn.
2 I'm very sorry, **I can't remember** / I'm not remembering your name.
3 Can you help me with my homework? I'm not understanding / **I don't understand** this question.
4 John **is having** / has a great time on holiday. Look at these pictures on his blog!
5 I'm afraid you can't borrow that book. **It belongs** / It is belonging to my sister and she **is reading** / reads it at the moment.
6 **I don't want to** / I'm not wanting to go out tonight. I'm too tired!
7 My brother **has** / is having so many hobbies! At the moment, he **is taking** / takes photos in the garden.
8 Sue isn't hearing / **can't hear** you at the moment. She **is having** / has a shower.

09▷ Complete the email from a university student using the correct form of the verbs in brackets.

To: William
From: Katy

Hi William,

I **1** _____ (**have**) a great time here in Leeds. The city is really big and I
2 _____ (**have**) so many interesting places to visit. I **3** _____ (**enjoy**) my
course so far and I really **4** _____ (**like**) my classmates. I **5** _____ (**stay**)
in one of the halls of residence this year, but next year I may move into an apartment with
some friends. I **6** _____ (**have got**) a job in a local restaurant so I can earn
some extra money. I **7** _____ (**work**) there three evenings a week from 7pm
untill midnight. It's fine, but at the moment I **8** _____ (**look**) for another job.
I **9** _____ (**want**) one that **10** _____ (**finish**) a bit earlier because
I need more sleep!

Write soon with your news,

Katy

10▷ Match the questions and short answers.

1 Is that your brother playing tennis over there? _____
2 Do you always get up so early? _____
3 Are your parents staying in a hotel? _____
4 Are you making chocolate cake? _____
5 Is your brother having a good time in Iceland? _____
6 Do you and your parents always eat together in the evenings? _____
7 Look at this picture of me as a young child. Am I wearing your gold necklace? _____
8 Do any of your school friends do taekwondo? _____

A No, I'm not.

B Yes, I do.

C Yes, you are.

D Yes, it is.

E No, we don't.

F Yes, they are.

G No, they don't.

H Yes, he is.

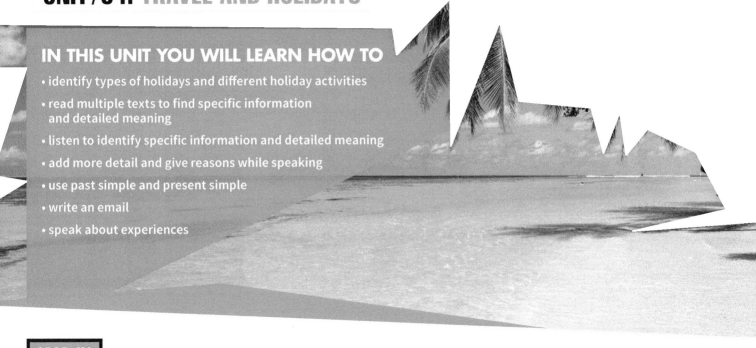

IN THIS UNIT YOU WILL LEARN HOW TO

• identify types of holidays and different holiday activities

• read multiple texts to find specific information
  and detailed meaning

• listen to identify specific information and detailed meaning

• add more detail and give reasons while speaking

• use past simple and present simple

• write an email

• speak about experiences

LEAD-IN

01 Look at the pictures. What are these types of holidays? Match the pictures with the type of holiday, A–D.

   A an adventure holiday   **B** a city break   **C** a language exchange   **D** a beach holiday

02▶ Label the pictures with the holiday activities.

visit water parks	go on day trips	go on cultural visits	go horse riding	try traditional food
visit beach resorts	see local attractions	stay with host families	go mountain climbing	
go on cycling tours	go shopping	see famous buildings		

03▶ In pairs, discuss which holiday activities from Exercise 2 you can do on the different types of holidays in Exercise 1.

04 ▶ You are going to read about some people who want to book a holiday. First, read the descriptions of eight different types of holiday. Which would be the best holiday for you?

In some exam reading tasks, you may be asked to complete a matching exercise where you match descriptions to people. First, identify key words and ideas for each person.
Then, match these words and ideas with the descriptions.

Ⓐ WILDLIFE EXPERIENCE

Come and learn about nature on our wildlife adventure holidays. Find out where your favourite animals live, what they eat and how to protect them. Our guides will show you local wildlife in its natural environment. Don't forget your camera!

Ⓑ FUN FAMILY HOLIDAYS

This is a great choice for families looking for fun on holiday. Choose from activities at zoos and water parks, as well as day trips to local attractions such as museums, art galleries and shopping centres. Accommodation and meals are all included, leaving you with more time to enjoy your favourite activities.

Ⓒ DELICIOUS FOOD TOURS

If you enjoy trying new food, you will love this holiday! This is the perfect chance to visit popular markets and restaurants with other food-lovers, attend cookery demonstrations and prepare your own delicious meals with the help of local chefs.

Ⓓ ADVENTURE HOLIDAYS

Are you looking for a real adventure in the great outdoors? Try one of our mountain climbing, horse riding or cycling tours! Our fully qualified activity instructors will share their knowledge of the area and entertain you with true stories about their past adventures. No previous experience is required, but you need to have lots of energy.

Ⓔ BEACH ESCAPE

This is the perfect holiday for people who simply want to relax. We offer luxury accommodation in our beach resorts, a variety of restaurants serving delicious local food and perfect cafes to relax and watch the sunset. Water sports, including snorkelling, windsurfing and sailing, are also available.

Ⓕ LANGUAGE EXCHANGE

Do you want to improve your language skills while experiencing life in another country? Our local host families will give you the chance to practise speaking the language, teach you how to cook traditional food and take you to the best local attractions. The Language Exchange holiday is a perfect way to make new friends and explore Europe.

Ⓖ SAILING EXPERIENCE

Whether you are a complete beginner or an experienced sailor, we can give you the perfect sailing experience! Learn the basics of sailing or more advanced techniques with our qualified sailing instructors.

Ⓗ CITY BREAKS

Do you enjoy visiting art galleries, museums or famous buildings? Do you want to visit other countries? On our cultural tours in Europe, you can learn about the history of the city you are visiting. Every day includes a different cultural visit.

05▷ Now, read what type of holiday each person wants to go on and read the holiday descriptions again. Then, choose the best holiday for each person.

TIP 05

Remember to read the information in the texts carefully. Some, but not all of the information may match.

0 Tom is 19 and is very active. He enjoys all kinds of sports and being outdoors. He has done a lot of water sports in the past, like sailing and windsurfing but he would like to try something different for his holiday this year. He went to the beach last year, but got bored after a few days.

Best holiday: ___D___

05.0 MINI TIP Does Tom like to relax on a beach or be more active? Does he want to do water sports or try something different?

1 Julia is 16 and would like to go on holiday with her best friend from school during the summer holidays. They want to travel to a new place, visit local attractions and try new food. Their parents will not allow their daughters to be in another country without any adults, but they will allow them to travel on their own. Julia and her friend both study Spanish at school and are planning to take a Spanish exam next year.

Best holiday: _____

05.1 MINI TIP Are Julia and her friend able to stay in a foreign country without their parents?

2 Charlie is 21 years old and has just finished university. He would like to spend the summer doing something interesting with some friends before they start looking for jobs. He prefers holidays in the countryside to holidays in cities or at the beach. He thinks that he would like to get a job working with animals in the future.

Best holiday: _____

05.2 MINI TIP What is the most important information about Charlie's interests?

3 Joanna is 32 and works as a teacher. She wants to book a holiday in August with her husband. She is usually very tired after a busy term at school and would like to go somewhere hot and near the sea. She wants to relax and not do very much.

Best holiday: _____

05.3 MINI TIP What are the two most important things Joanna is looking for on her holiday?

4 Roger is 50 and wants to book a holiday for his wife and two children. They would like to do some cultural activities, such as visiting museums and art galleries, but also some fun activities to entertain the children. They also love shopping.

Best holiday: _____

05.4 MINI TIP Does Roger just want to visit museums and galleries?

06▷ In pairs, discuss the questions.

1 Which holiday from Exercise 4 would you *most* like to go on? Which is the most interesting to you? Why?

2 Which holiday from Exercise 4 would you *not* like to go on? Why?

LISTENING: INTERVIEW TASK

07▷ You are going to listen to a radio interview with a student called Anna, who has recently taken part in a summer cultural exchange programme. First, look at the example question and the answer options, and read the Bullet Box. Then, listen to Part 1 of the interview.

In some Listening exam tasks, you may be asked to listen to an interview. In these tasks, you should:

- identify the key words in the question or statement.
- identify key words in the three multiple-choice options. You may hear all the key words but only one answers the question or completes the statement.
- remember that you may also not hear the exact words that you see in the question or options.

0 Why did Anna decide to go on a language exchange programme in Spain?

A She is good at sports.

B She studies Spanish and not French.

C She wanted to go somewhere new.

Answer: C

08▷ Now, read Part 1 of the interview and the highlighted parts. In pairs, discuss why C is the correct answer in Exercise 7.

Well, students can travel to France or Spain on a language exchange, or to the USA on a sports or music exchange. I didn't go to the USA because I'm not very good at sports. However, I study French and Spanish at school, so I had two options. I've been to France before, so I decided to go to Spain instead.

09▷ Listen to Part 2 of the radio interview and answer the questions. For each question, choose the correct answer, A, B or C.

07

1 Where did Anna's host family live?
  A in an apartment
  B in a house
  C on a farm

2 How long did Anna stay with her host family?
  A two weeks
  B three weeks
  C four weeks

3 How old do students have to be to take part in the language exchange programme?
  A 13
  B over 14
  C 16

4 Students can go on the language exchange programme if
  A they are 16 or over and their parents allow them.
  B they study a language like French or Spanish at school.
  C they play in a school sports team or in the school orchestra.

5 Anna thinks that her Spanish
  A hasn't improved.
  B has improved a little
  C has improved a lot.

SPEAKING: ADDING MORE DETAIL AND GIVING REASONS

10▷ Look at the sentences from Anna's interview in Exercises 8-9. Match the two halves of the sentence.

1 I didn't go to the USA
2 The family had a daughter who was my age called Carmen,
3 <u>As</u> I love animals
4 Carmen spoke really good English,

A <u>so</u> we had lots of fun together.
B <u>so</u> I was worried that I wouldn't improve my Spanish.
C <u>because</u> I'm not very good at sports.
D it was a really good experience for me.

11▷ Read the Tip Box and answer the questions.

1 Which of the <u>underlined words</u> in the sentences in Exercise 10 come before the reason?

2 Which of the <u>underlined words</u> in the sentences in Exercise 10 come before the result?

TIP 11

One good way to give more details when you are talking in the Speaking exam is to give reasons. Use *as*, *so* and *because* to help you connect ideas. Notice the differences in Exercise 10 with the structures and order.

12▷ In pairs, answer the questions using the structures in the Useful Language box to explain your reasons for your answers.

1 If you were on a language exchange, would you like to stay with a host family or in a hotel more? Why?

2 Where do you usually go on holiday? Why?

3 What do you like more – holidays with your friends or holidays with your family? Why?

4 What's better: a beach holiday or a city break? Why?

5 What's better: an adventure holiday or a language exchange? Why?

GRAMMAR: PAST SIMPLE AND PRESENT SIMPLE

13▷ Read Part 1 of the interview with Anna from Exercise 8 again and answer the questions.

Well, students **1** _can travel_ to France or Spain on a language exchange, or to the USA on a sports or music exchange. I **2** _didn't go_ to the USA because **3** _I'm not_ very good at sports. However, I **4** _study_ French and Spanish at school, so I **5** _had_ two options. I've been to France before, so I **6** _decided to_ go to Spain instead.

1 Which number describes a present state? _____

2 Which numbers describe a habit or a regular activity? _____

3 Which numbers describe an action completed in the past? _____

14▷ Match the sentences 1–3 in Exercise 13 with the tenses 1 and 2. Then, read the Grammar box to check your answers.

1 Present simple _____   2 Past simple _____

Present simple	Past simple
We use the present simple to talk about states in the present: *I'm (not) good at sports.* We also use the present simple to talk about habits and things people do regularly: *I go to French lessons twice a week.*	We use the past simple to talk about an action completed in the past: *I decided to go …* We also use the past simple for past states that may or may not still be true: *Seville was very nice (when I visited it).*
Negative: add *NOT* for states (*I'm not good at sports.*) and *DO NOT* for actions (*I do not/don't study French.*)	**Negative:** add *NOT* for states (*Seville was not very nice.*) and *DID NOT* for actions (*I did not/didn't decide to go.*)
Questions: The word order changes for states (*Are you good at sports?*) and we also add *DO* for actions (*Do you study French?*)	**Questions:** The word order changes for states (*Was Seville nice?*) and we also add *DID* for actions (*Did you decide to go?*)
Note: For regular verbs, the third person (*he / she / it*) changes from the infinitive form to *-s* or *-(i)es*. There are more changes for irregular verbs.	**Note:** For regular verbs, there is no change to the infinitive form for the past simple. However, there are changes for irregular verbs.

15▷ Look at the verb form mistakes 1–6 in the summary. Rewrite the verbs, 1–6, correctly.

Anna **1** study French and Spanish at school at the moment. Last summer, she **2** goes to Spain on a language exchange where she **3** stayed with a family in a village. Anna now **4** thought that the language exchange programme **5** was a good experience for her although she **6** wasn't much better at Spanish now than before.

16▷ You are going to read an email from your friend Simon about his holiday. Take two minutes to read the email quickly and answer the questions.

1 Where did he go?

2 Why was this holiday different to his trips before?

To: Tony
From: Simon

Hi Tony,

I **1** _____ (**go**) to Madrid for my last holiday – it **2** _____ (**be**) great!
On the first day, I **3** _____ (**visit**) some of the famous sights here including the Prado museum and the Royal Palace. It is different to my usual holidays. Normally, I **4** _____ (**go**) to hot places and relax on the beach. At the moment, it's the opposite and it is quite cold here. On my second day, I **5** _____ (**go**) shopping and **6** _____ (**buy**) some souvenirs. That night it **7** _____ (**be**) really interesting because I **8** _____ (**eat**) in a Spanish restaurant. I usually **9** _____ (**not try**) new food when I go on holiday, but I am very happy that I **10** _____ (**do**) this time. I **11** _____ (**try**) a traditional meal of soup, vegetables and meat. It **12** _____ (**be**) delicious. It **13** _____ (**be**) only a short holiday, but I really enjoyed it.

I **14** _____ (**take**) lots of photos. What **15** _____ (**do**) you do on your holiday?
Where **16** _____ (**do**) you go?
Simon

17▷ Read the email again. Then, complete the email using the correct form of the verbs in brackets.

18▷ Look again at Simon's email. In the table below, tick ✓ the features in his email that he uses.

Feature	✓ ?
1 He uses a greeting to start the email.	
2 He says where he went on holiday.	
3 He says how he travelled there.	
4 He says how long he stayed.	
5 He says what he did on holiday.	
6 He says what he usually does on holiday.	
7 He asks about his friend's last holiday.	
8 He asks about his friend's next holiday.	
9 He finishes with his name at the end.	

19▷ Now, read the task and write your email.

Your friend, Hannah, wants to know about your last holiday. She wants to know where you went and what you did.

Write an email to your friend. In your email you should:

• say where you went.

• say what you did there.

• ask your friend about his/her last holiday.

• Write 150–175 words.

20 ▷ In pairs, compare your emails from Exercise 19. Complete the table to see what your partner did well and what you think needs to be improved.

Feature	✓ ?
1 Uses a good structure – greeting to start the email and ends with his/her name.	
2 Says where he/she went on holiday.	
3 Says what he/she did on holiday.	
4 Asks his/her friend about his/her last holiday.	
5 He/She only talks about the information in the instructions.	
6 He/She uses the correct number of words	

SPEAKING: EXPERIENCES

21 ▷ In pairs, discuss the questions.

1 What did you find most interesting about Anna's story in Exercises 7 and 9?
2 Have you had a similar experience to Anna? What happened? Describe your experience.
3 If you haven't had a similar experience to Anna, would you like to? Why / Why not?

22 ▷ Read the task. What would you say? Spend one minute preparing what you could say and make some notes.

Describe a trip you really liked.

You should say:

- where you went.
- what you did on the trip.
- why you went.
- why you liked it so much.

TIP 22

It is important to know that there is a difference between a *trip*, a *journey* and the verb to *travel*.
Trip = a journey, a holiday or to travel for business or study.

23 ▷ Now, do the task. Use the bullet box to help you.

- Work in pairs.
- Student A – speak for 1–2 minutes about your own travel experiences.
- Student B – listen.
- Swap roles.

◉ **Exam speaking task – talk about your own experiences**

- In this part of the Speaking exam, it is important that you are able to speak about your personal experience in relation to the topic.
- The examiner will give you **one minute** to prepare – it is very important that you use this time to think about your answer.
- You will be given a *task card* to read – this has written prompts. You must follow all the instructions on the *task card*. Use the prompts to structure your answers.
- You will be given a pencil and paper to make notes if you like – do **NOT** write on the task card. Notes can help you remember the key ideas you want to say.
- Do **NOT** just give very short answers – they need to be long and developed answers.
- Remember, you need to speak for **1–2 minutes** – try to speak for two minutes or just under.
- Remember to give examples and reasons.
- Be prepared to answer more questions on the same topic in the next phase of the exam.

GRAMMAR AND VOCABULARY

01▷ Complete the sentences using the types of holidays in the box.

> a city break   a beach holiday   a family holiday   a language exchange   an adventure holiday

1 You can do lots of activities like cycling and horse riding on _____ .
2 My friends want to go on _____ , but I don't enjoy relaxing all the time.
3 I went on _____ to Paris. It was interesting to visit all the museums.
4 My sister is going on _____ and will stay with a host family in Italy.
5 I went on _____ with my parents and we camped by a lake.

02▷ Complete the table using the holiday activities in the box.

> visit water parks   go on day trips   see local attractions   go on cultural visits
> go horse riding   go on cycling tours   visit beach resorts   go mountain climbing
> stay with host families   try traditional food   see famous buildings   go shopping

city break	adventure holiday	beach holiday	language exchange

03▷ Complete the sentences using the holiday activities in the box.

> visit water parks   go on day trips   go shopping   go horse riding
> go on a cycling tour   go on a cultural visit   visit a beach resort
> go mountain climbing   visit local attractions   stay with a host family

1 We often _____ in the airport where you can buy things more cheaply.
2 When I visit my aunt, we often _____ in the countryside. I love animals.
3 You can _____ like a 9th century castle in my town.
4 Families like to _____ when the weather is hot so they can cool down.
5 You can _____ by coach to the countryside from the city.
6 It is often cheaper to _____ in their own home than in a hotel.
7 If you are fit, a good way to see more of a country is to _____ .
8 You shouldn't _____ alone as it can be a dangerous sport.
9 When you _____ in a city, you have the chance to see museums and art galleries.
10 If you _____ you can enjoy being by the sea, and do a variety of activities, like surfing and water-skiing.

04 ▶ Complete the sentences using the words in the box.

boring	local	natural	traditional	famous
cultural	fun	popular	delicious	interesting

1 The USA is a very _____ country to visit. Last year, it had over a million visitors.

2 I think that it is more _____ to go on holiday with friends than with family because friends are interested in doing similar activities.

3 I would prefer to see animals in their _____ environment than in a zoo.

4 If you go on a language exchange programme, you can learn a lot about the _____ area where your host family lives.

5 A lot of people like to go to the beach for holidays, but I find it _____ .

6 I prefer to do _____ activities on holiday, like visiting museums and art galleries than to spend all my time on the beach.

7 Barcelona has a lot of _____ buildings. Many of them were designed by the artist Antoni Gaudi.

8 On the last night of my holiday, I ate the most _____ meal in a restaurant by the sea.

9 The Eiffel Tour is the most _____ building in Paris – people all over the world know what it looks like.

10 I love to eat _____ food when I go on holiday. I don't always like it, but it is fun to try it.

05 ▶ Read the conversation and underline the correct answer.

A **1 Do you like / You like** going on holiday?

B Yes, **2 I do / I did**. I always have a great time on holiday with my family.

A I do, too. Where **3 did you usually go / do you usually go**?

B Usually we go on a beach holiday but last summer we **4 go / went** on a city break.

A What **5 do you do / did you do** there?

B Well, because my parents **6 enjoy / enjoys** going to the theatre, **7 we all go / we all went** to see a play by a famous British writer.

A **8 Is it / Was it** good? I **9 not really like / don't really like** plays. I think they are boring.

B I thought that, too, but this one **10 wasn't / didn't** boring at all. It was really fun.

0 6 ▷ Complete the email using the correct form of the verbs in brackets.

To: Tony
From: Sarah

Hi Tony,

I **1** _____ (**go**) to Germany with my family last year last February.
My family and I **2** _____ (**not like**) beach holidays, we
3 _____ (**decide**) to go to Berlin for a weekend.
Usually on holiday, I **4** _____ (**enjoy**) visiting lots of famous museums
and monuments but we **5** _____ (**not have**) time to see everything, so
we just **6** _____ (**see**) the main ones, like the Berlin Wall and the
Brandenburg Gate. In my opinion, they **7** _____ (**be**) both very
interesting monuments. I **8** _____ (**learn**) about them at school last year.
We **9** _____ (**feel**) cold a lot of the time because it
10 _____ (**be**) the middle of winter.
Where **11** _____ (**you / like**) going on holiday?
12 _____ (**you / prefer**) city breaks in winter or beach holidays in the
summer?
Take care,
Sarah

0 7 ▷ Match the two halves of the sentence.

1 I go to French lessons
2 The weather in Stockholm wasn't very nice
3 I'm not good at sport
4 Did you decide to
5 Are you good

A but I enjoy hiking and horse riding.
B stay with a host family?
C at sailing?
D twice a week.
E when we visited in December.

0 8 ▷ Choose the best answer, A, B or C.

1 I didn't go on the language exchange *because* / *so* my language level wasn't high enough.
2 *As* / *So* we enjoy kayaking, we decided to go on an adventure holiday this year.
3 The host family spoke English really well *so* / *because* I wasn't worried that we wouldn't be able to communicate.
4 We prefer city breaks *so* / *because* we enjoy exploring new places.
5 *So* / *As* my parents enjoy trying traditional food, they went on a food tour.

IN THIS UNIT YOU WILL LEARN HOW TO

- identify different ingredients and categories of food
- use singular and plural countable and uncountable nouns
- give a description of a process
- speak about a meal you enjoy

0 1 ▷ Look at the pictures. Match the countries in the box with the pictures of different food.

| Saudi Arabia | the United Kingdom | China | Italy | Brazil |

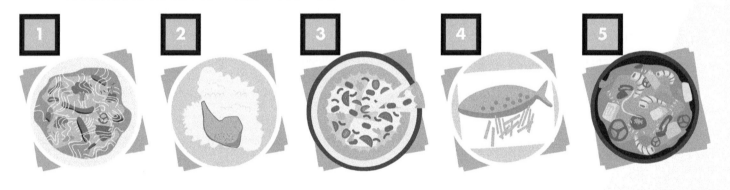

1 **2** **3** **4** **5**

VOCABULARY AND SPEAKING

0 2 ▷ Match the ingredients 1–5 with the dishes A–E.

1	Beef Chow Mein	**A**	tomatoes	cheese	flour for bread		
2	Al Kabsa	**B**	tomatoes	fish	prawns	rice	coconut milk
3	Pizza	**C**	fish	potatoes			
4	Fish and chips	**D**	meat	noodles	oil	garlic	broccoli
5	Moqueca	**E**	chicken	rice	tomato	onion	

0 3 ▷ In pairs, read and discuss the following questions.

1 Have you tried any of these dishes in Exercise 2?
2 What is your favourite food from your country?
3 What food is popular in your country?

0 4 ▷ Look at the photos below. Which do you think you might see at a food festival? Discuss your ideas with a partner.

Food stalls

Traditional activities

Famous chefs

Arts and crafts

Fairground rides

0 5 ▷ You are going to read an article about the Chinese food festival in London. Skim the text once quickly. Which of the ideas in Exercise 4 does it mention?

CHINESE FOOD FESTIVAL IN LONDON

This year, the Chinese food festival is at the **South Bank Riverside Walkway** by the **River Thames in London.**

The three-day food festival celebrates real Chinese cooking and dishes from other countries. You can taste wonderful food at the many food stalls, and watch famous chefs showing you how to make some tasty dishes.

All the family can come and enjoy food, traditional Chinese performances and try Chinese arts and crafts.

The festival starts on 25th September and tickets are free! Just go to our website and download your free ticket.

06 ▷ Read the article again and the sentences, 1–6. The information in bold in the sentences is incorrect. Correct the sentences by choosing the best answer, A, B or C.

1 The Chinese food festival is in London **every year**.
   A True   B False   C Not Given

2 The festival **only** includes Chinese cooking.
   A True   B False   C Not Given

3 You can **learn** to make some of the Chinese food at the festival.
   A True   B False   C Not Given

4 **Children** can come to the festival.
   A True   B False   C Not Given

5 The festival is **only** about cooking.
   A True   B False   C Not Given

6 If you don't download a ticket, you **must pay** to enter on the day.
   A True   B False   C Not Given

TIP 06

Answer the questions about the Chinese food festival. The words in **bold** will help you to choose the correct answer.

You need to be careful that the answer is exactly what it says in the text.

06.1 MINI TIP Does the text say that the festival happens every year?

LISTENING: MATCHING

07 ▷ You are going to listening to Mark and Jane discussing the food festival. What is the main topic of their conversation? Listen and choose the best answer, A, B or C.

A The activities they want to see there.
B The friends they will invite to the festival.
C The reasons their other friends can't go.

08 ▷ Listen again and match the people, 1–6 with the reasons, A–H.

1 Marco   A is going sightseeing

               B can't afford to go

2 Mohammed   C is working

3 Pierre   D is going to a restaurant

4 Hang Yie   E is helping someone

               F is doing something with their flatmate

5 Lucy   G is in a different country

6 Larissa   H is studying

TIP 08

Be careful. There are more reasons than people, so you won't use all the letters.

08.A MINI TIP What does 'sightseeing' mean?

08.B MINI TIP If you can't afford something, what don't you have?

08.F MINI TIP Where does a 'flatmate' live?

09 ▷ Listen again and check your answers.

TIP 09

Make sure you listen for all of the information.

10 Match the food words in the box with the pictures.

| lamb | onion | pasta | flour | salmon | garlic | carrot | rice | spring onion |

11 Complete the table using the food words from Exercise 10.

Meat	Vegetables	Fish/Seafood	Carbohydrates	Other ingredients
chicken	broccoli	shrimps	potatoes	salt
beef			noodles	pepper

12 In pairs, add some more food words to the table.

13 Match the verbs for preparing food with the photos.

| boil | chop | cut | fold | fry | mix | roll |

1 4 ▶ You are going to listen to a chef giving a cooking demonstration. Listen to the introduction. Which recipe is he going to cook? Choose the best answer, A, B or C.

09

noodles

mooncakes

dumplings

1 5 ▶ Listen to the second part of the chef's demonstration. Complete the descriptions of the diagram using the words in the box.

10

| boil   chop(x2)   cut   fold   mix(x2)   roll |

TIP 15

You will not always hear the exact same information spoken in the Listening as written in the exercises. You will need to listen for the specific information you want.

1 You need to
_____ water
with flour to make the cases.

2 You need to
_____ the
cabbage to make the filling.

3 You _____
the meat and cabbage
by hand.

4 You need to
_____ the
spring onions and shrimps
into small pieces.

5 You need to
_____ the
dough in to 20 equal pieces
to make the cases.

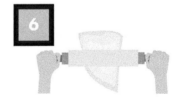

6 Then you _____
the dough into flat cases.

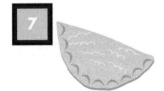

7 You _____ the
dough into half-moon shapes.

8 You _____ the
dumplings three times and
they are ready to eat.

Before you listen, it is a good idea to see if you can predict the information.

1 6 Read the list of ingredients. Which of the ingredients did the chef use in the recipe in Exercise 15? Complete the table using the words in the box.

(an) apple (a) cabbage (some) flour (some) meat (some) milk onion(s) orange(s) potato(es) (some) rice (some) salt shrimp(s) (some) water

Countable (singular)	Countable (plural)	Uncountable
an apple	(some) potatoes	(some) flour

1 7 Complete the sentences using *a / an* or *some*.

1 For singular countable nouns, we put _____ before the word e.g. _____ cabbage.

2 For plural countable nouns, we can put _____ before the word and we usually add an 's' e.g. _____ dumplings.

3 For uncountable nouns, we put _____ before the word e.g. _____ milk.

1 8 Read the sentences and complete headings in the table.

	1 _____ nouns	2 _____ nouns
+	*I have **some** apples.*	*I have **some** rice.*
–	*I don't have **any** cabbages.*	*I don't have **any** milk.*
?	*Do you have **any** onions?*	*Do you have **any** meat?*
A lot of (+)	*We have **a lot of** sweets in the cupboard.*	*We have **a lot of** ice cream in the freezer.*
Much/Many (? –)	*How **many** carrots do we need?* *He doesn't have **many** friends.*	*How **much** water do I put in?* *You don't need to add **much** oil.*

1 9 Look at the questions about eating habits. Write three more questions about eating habits using the grammar in Exercises 16–18.

Food questionnaire

*Do you eat **a lot of** ice cream?*
*Have you ever eaten **a** mooncake?*
*How **much** water do you drink each day?*
*Are there **any** foods you don't like?*

1 _____

2 _____

3 _____

2 0 In pairs, ask and answer the questions.

21▷ Read the instructions about making a Korean dish called Bulgogi and look at the pictures. First, put the pictures A–F in the correct order.

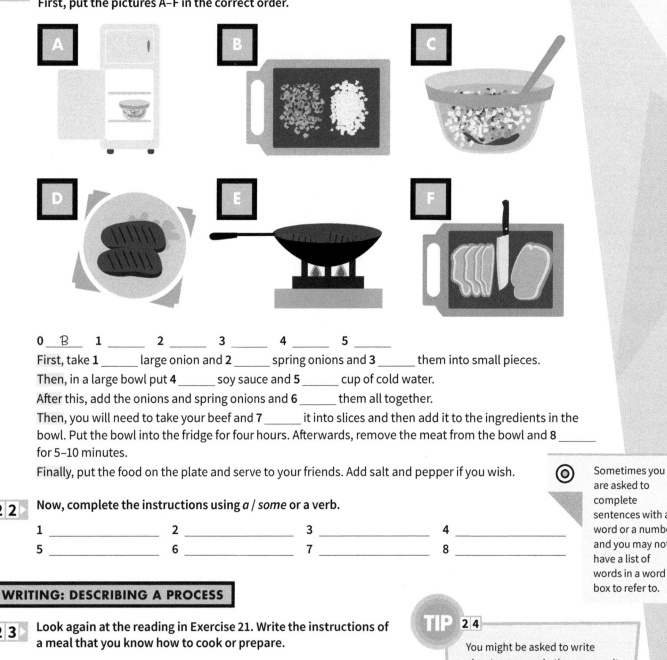

0 __B__   1 _____   2 _____   3 _____   4 _____   5 _____

First, take **1** _____ large onion and **2** _____ spring onions and **3** _____ them into small pieces.

Then, in a large bowl put **4** _____ soy sauce and **5** _____ cup of cold water.

After this, add the onions and spring onions and **6** _____ them all together.

Then, you will need to take your beef and **7** _____ it into slices and then add it to the ingredients in the bowl. Put the bowl into the fridge for four hours. Afterwards, remove the meat from the bowl and **8** _____ for 5–10 minutes.

Finally, put the food on the plate and serve to your friends. Add salt and pepper if you wish.

22▷ Now, complete the instructions using *a* / *some* or a verb.

1 _____   2 _____   3 _____   4 _____

5 _____   6 _____   7 _____   8 _____

◎ Sometimes you are asked to complete sentences with a word or a number and you may not have a list of words in a word box to refer to.

WRITING: DESCRIBING A PROCESS

23▷ Look again at the reading in Exercise 21. Write the instructions of a meal that you know how to cook or prepare.

_____
_____
_____
_____
_____
_____
_____
_____
_____
_____
_____

TIP 24

You might be asked to write about a process in the exam so it is important to practise linking your ideas together. Look at the sequencing words highlighted in Exercise 21 to see how the parts of the instructions are linked.

2 4 Read the text and choose the best answer, A, B, C or D.

 Sometimes you will need to choose from a list of words to complete the gaps in a text.

I don't usually like **1** _____ meals and because I live alone, I often go **2** _____ restaurants or eat fast food in the week. **3** _____ the weekend, I have more **4** _____ time, so I usually cook my favourite meal. My **5** _____ meal is chicken curry with rice and vegetables. I don't have an oven, so I **6** _____ the chicken on its own in a pan and **7** _____ the rice in water. I like this meal so much that sometimes I also order it in restaurants. I sometimes also eat it four times a week! It is very popular **8** _____ my country, too. I think a lot of people like it because it is healthy and easy to make. You can also change the recipe so it is spicy or not, so everybody can enjoy it.

1 A cooking	**B** cook	**C** do	**D** doing
2 A in	**B** at	**C** to	**D** for
3 A For	**B** At	**C** In	**D** With
4 A extra	**B** free	**C** off	**D** hobby
5 A lovely	**B** liked	**C** favourite	**D** popular
6 A fold	**B** mix	**C** fry	**D** chop
7 A fry	**B** cut	**C** roll	**D** boil
8 A in	**B** with	**C** at	**D** on

2 5 In pairs, you are going to talk about a meal that you enjoy. Use the information in Exercise 24 to help you.

In your talk, you should speak about the following:

- who prepares it for you.
- when you eat it.
- why you like it.

2 6 Use the information from this unit to write an essay about a meal that is popular in your country or one that you enjoy.

In your essay, you should include:

- what ingredients you need.
- the instructions about how you make it.
- the reasons why it is popular.

MODEL ANSWER

My favourite meal is Spaghetti Bolognese. To make Spaghetti Bolognese, you need minced beef, onions, garlic, a can of chopped tomatoes and pasta. First of all, you need to chop the onions and garlic and fry them until they are soft. After this, you add the minced beef and cook it until it is brown. Next, you need to add the chopped tomatoes and continue cooking. While it is cooking, you need to boil some water. When the water is ready, add the pasta and boil it for about 11 minutes. After this, put the pasta on plates and add the sauce. Finally, put some cheese on top and salt and pepper if you want and it is ready to eat.

Spaghetti Bolognese is my favourite dish because it is simple to make and is very tasty. I think that it is popular because it tastes so good. There are also many different ways to make it and you can use more vegetables or different types of pasta, so everyone can enjoy it.

GRAMMAR AND VOCABULARY

0 1 ▷ Match the different foods in the box to the photos.

| beef | lettuce | duck | lobster | spaghetti | salmon | garlic | cauliflower |

1

2

3

4

5

6

7

8

0 2 ▷ Complete the table using the words in the box.

| beef | lettuce | duck | lobster | spaghetti | salmon | carrot | garlic | cauliflower |

Meat	Vegetables	Fish/Seafood	Carbohydrates

0 3 Match the cooking methods 1–5 to the definitions A–E.

1 bake

2 boil

3 chop

4 fry

5 mix

A to cook food in water.

B to cut something into small pieces.

C to cook something such as bread or a cake with dry heat in the oven.

D to put two or more ingredients together.

E to cook something in hot oil or fat.

0 4 Complete the chart below using the words in the box.

some   any   a   an

Before singular countable nouns we use **1** _____ before a consonant and **2** _____ before a vowel.

• I have **3** _____ sandwich for lunch.

• I had **4** _____ apple for a snack today.

In positive sentences, with plural and uncountable nouns we use **5** _____ .

• I have got **6** _____ juice in the fridge.

• There are **7** _____ oranges in the cupboard.

In questions and negative sentences with countable and uncountable nouns, we use **8** _____ .

• Are there **9** _____ tomatoes?

• Is there **10** _____ fish on the menu?

In offers and requests, we use **11** _____ .

• Can I have **12** _____ water, please?

• Would you like **13** _____ tea?

0 5 Read the sentences in the chart and underline the correct answer.

We use **1 a lot of** / **many** with positive and negative sentences with countable and uncountable nouns.

• We have **2 much** / **a lot of** oranges to eat because we have an orange tree in our garden.

• We don't have **3 a lot of** / **many** fruit to eat in winter.

We use **4 much** / **many** with questions and negatives with countable nouns.

• How **5 much** / **many** lemons do you need for the recipe?

• There aren't **6 much** / **many** cauliflowers in the shop.

We use **7 many** / **much** with questions and negatives with uncountable nouns.

• How **8 many** / **much** coffee is there in the cupboard?

• There isn't **9 many** / **much** sugar in the dish.

0 6 ▷ **Choose the best answer, A, B or C.**

1 Could you go to the shop? There isn't _____ milk in the fridge.

   A some   **B** many   **C** much

2 How _____ eggs do we need to make the cake?

   A many   **B** much   **C** a lot of

3 There are _____ potatoes in the cupboard, so we could make chips.

   A much   **B** any   **C** a lot of

4 Do you have _____ spaghetti?

   A any   **B** many   **C** a

5 I think that we have _____ carrots in the fridge.

   A much   **B** some   **C** any

6 I would like _____ fish, please.

   A some   **B** much   **C** many

7 How _____ sugar would you like in your coffee?

   A many   **B** much   **C** any

8 There aren't _____ vegetables in the shop, just cauliflower and lettuce.

   A any   **B** many   **C** much

9 We don't have _____ beef left. Everyone ate it. Would you like chicken instead?

   A any   **B** many   **C** much

10 There are _____ different salads on the menu. I don't know which one to choose.

   A any   **B** much   **C** a lot of

0 7 ▷ **Read the narrative and choose the best answer, A, B or C.**

My **1** _____ food is pizza. I like **2** _____ pizzas because they are very easy to prepare. If you want to **3** _____ your own pizza, all you need to do is make the bread for the base. This is called the dough. You can **4** _____ tomatoes and cheese and **5** _____ other ingredients on top. You then **6** _____ it in the oven for 10 to 15 minutes until it is ready to eat. If you don't feel like making pizza, you can buy **7** _____ pizza from your local supermarket and just put it in the oven when you get home. Nowadays, **8** _____ of people are so busy that they don't have time to cook at home or they like to have a rest **9** _____ the weekend. These people often also eat pizza, but they go **10** _____ a take-away restaurant and buy a pizza that has already been made.

1 A best	**B** lovely	**C** favourite
2 A eating	**B** eat	**C** ate
3 A get	**B** have	**C** make
4 A mix	**B** fold	**C** add
5 A a lot	**B** many	**C** much
6 A cook	**B** boil	**C** fry
7 A much	**B** some	**C** a
8 A much	**B** a lot	**C** many
9 A at	**B** in	**C** for
10 A in	**B** for	**C** to

08 ▸ **Read the instructions about making an Arabian cauliflower recipe and look at the pictures. Then, match the pictures to the instructions.**

A While the cauliflower is boiling, chop some garlic.

B Add the mixture of paste, garlic and lemon juice to the cauliflower.

C Next, add the garlic to some special mixture called tahini paste and some lemon juice.

D First, take a large cauliflower and cut the leaves off so that you only have the white part.

E Mix the paste, the lemon juice and the garlic together.

F Next, take the cauliflower and place it in boiling water.

G Finally, cover the dish and put it in the fridge until you are ready to eat it.

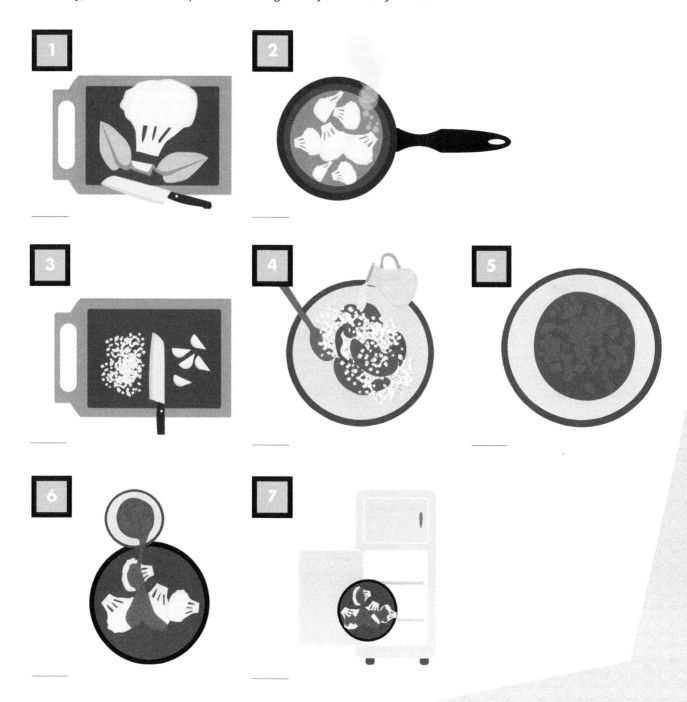

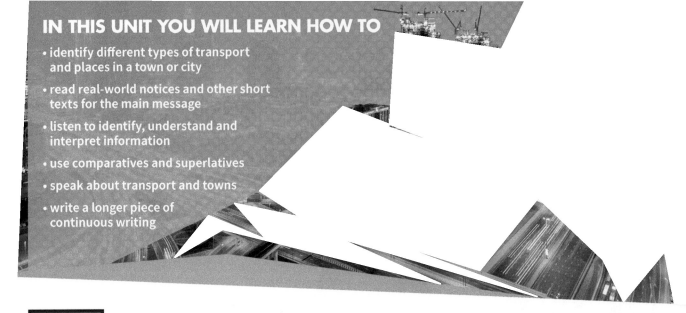

IN THIS UNIT YOU WILL LEARN HOW TO

- identify different types of transport and places in a town or city
- read real-world notices and other short texts for the main message
- listen to identify, understand and interpret information
- use comparatives and superlatives
- speak about transport and towns
- write a longer piece of continuous writing

0 1 ▶ Match the words in the box with the photos 1–5.

| statue castle stadium tower bridge |

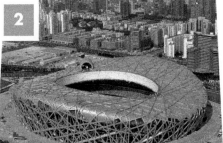

0 2 ▶ Look at the photos in Exercise 1 again. What are the names of the places and which countries do they come from?

0 3 ▶ What other famous buildings or monuments can you name, and which cities are they in? Are there any famous buildings or monuments in your city or town?

READING AND VOCABULARY

04 ▶ Complete the table with the correct words. Some words can be used twice.

square	motorway	motorbike	ticket	platform	post office

shopping centre   car park   library   sports centre   restaurant
coach   cafe   police station   department store   the underground

Places in a city	Travel and transport

05 ▶ Read the signs and notices. Add the words in blue to the table in Exercise 4.

◉ In some Reading exam questions, you will read some very short real-world texts, such as signs, messages, postcards, notes, emails or labels. You will need to work out the main idea of the text. Read the whole text and decide what the key words are to help you understand what the text says.

1

PARKING **FOR** SUPERMARKET **CUSTOMERS ONLY**
Free for two hours – after that £2 an hour.

2

Hi Tom,
Jim and I are playing football in the park today. Do you want to join us? We'll get on the bus at the town centre at 12:30pm. Let me know,
Harry

3

Trains **travelling north out of this** station **are delayed because of heavy snow.**

4

To: Su
From: Lee
Subject: Holiday Plans

Reply   Forward

I just checked and there are seats available on the flight we want. Let's book them soon before the price gets too expensive!

5

Hi Deon,
I went sightseeing around the city today on an open top bus. We visited the museum and the castle along the way. We're going on a boat trip tomorrow and we'll be back home on Friday.
George

6

MILLTOWN STATION

Bicycles should be left in the bicycle stands only. For advice, please speak to a member of staff, who can give more details.

7

Alice, how are you going to the theatre tonight? It's close enough for me to walk but Tim's going by car and he's offered to drive me. Let him know if you want him to drive you, too. Sonia

0 6 ▷ **Read the signs and messages again in Exercise 5. Choose the correct answer, A, B or C.**

1 What does the supermarket notice say?
  A You can pay £2 to leave your car in the supermarket car park all day.
  B Supermarket customers can only park here for 2 hours at a time.
  C You don't need to pay if you finish shopping within 2 hours.

2 Why did Harry write this message?
  A To give Tom and Jim instructions on how to get to the park.
  B To invite Tom to play football with him and Jim.
  C To find out what time Tom would like to play football.

3 What is the notice telling passengers?
  A They should wait for news about the weather before travelling.
  B Some passengers will be late today because of the weather.
  C The station is closed until the weather improves.

4 What does Lee suggest?
  A To book the flights as soon as possible.
  B To choose a less expensive flight.
  C To change the date of his and Su's flight.

5 What does George say?
  A His sightseeing trip included a visit to a museum and castle.
  B He visited the castle and museum after going on the boat trip
  C He hopes to do a boat trip and an open bus tour before returning home.

6 What are train passengers told at the station?
  A They must not leave bikes at the station.
  B Cycle parking is only for members of station staff.
  C If they need to know more, they can ask someone who works there.

7 What should Alice do?
  A Contact Tim if she would like a lift to the theatre.
  B Tell Sonia what her travel plans are for this evening.
  C Let Tim or Sonia know if she's going to the theatre.

06.1 MINI TIP The options all contain similar words, and they all use words from the notice. You need to pay close attention to the main idea of the notice, and find the option that matches that meaning.

06.2 MINI TIP Always read the question carefully to see which option is correct. There is information in the message about where and when they will play football, but this was not why Harry wrote the message.

LISTENING: GAP-FILL

0 7 ▷ **You will hear Part 1 of some information about a new shopping centre. While you listen, circle the words and numbers that you hear.**

11

7am	Thursday	£2.50
10am	356	£3.00
6pm	635	£3.50
8pm	790	£15.00
Tuesday	729	
Wednesday	£2.00	

08 ▶ Listen again to Part 1 of the information and complete the text with the missing information.

🎵 11

> **Northfields' shopping centre information**
>
> Name of architect who designed Northfields: **1** John _____
>
> Address and postcode: Forest Drive, **2** _____.
>
> Opening hours: 10am to 6pm
>
> Late night shopping until 8pm on **3** _____.
>
> **Transport**
>
> By car – free car park
>
> By bus – there are **4** _____ buses.
>
> Underground – From the town centre it only takes **5** _____.

In this type of Listening exam task, always read the questions carefully first, so you know what specific information you need to listen for. Information may include a day of the week, a price, a spelling, a number or a postcode.

Make sure you practise the alphabet often so you have no trouble with spelling questions.

09 ▶ You are going to listen to Part 2 of the information. Before you listen, match the phrases with the diagrams.

next to	on the left of	opposite	between	on the right of

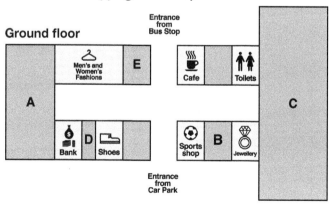

10 ▶ Now listen to Part 2 of some information about a new shopping centre. Look at the map and the list of shops. Match the shops with the correct letter, A–F.

🎵 12

1 cinema _____
2 supermarket _____
3 Green's department store _____

4 pharmacy _____
5 book store _____
6 mobile phone shop _____

Northfields' shopping centre map

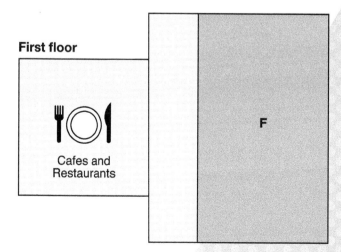

1 1 Compare your answers to Exercise 10 with a partner. Then, listen again and check.

🎵 12

1 2 Work in pairs. Ask and answer questions about the map in Exercise 10.

Examples:

A *Where can I buy a tennis racket?*

B *At the sports shop. It's on the ground floor opposite the cafe.*

A *Where's the bank?*

B *It's between the department store and the mobile phone shop.*

GRAMMAR: COMPARATIVES AND SUPERLATIVES

1 3 Read the Grammar table. Then, write the comparative and superlative forms of the adjectives in the box.

	Comparative	Superlative
One syllable	**+er**	**+est**
small	smaller	smallest
quick	quicker	quickest
(consonant / vowel / consonant)	**double last letter and +er**	
big	bigger	biggest
sad	sadder	saddest
Two or more syllables	**+ more**	**+ the most**
expensive	more expensive (than)	most expensive
important	more important (than)	most important
(Two syllables +y)	**+ier**	**+iest**
easy	easier	easiest
happy	happier	happiest
Irregular		
good	better	best
bad	worse	worst
far	further	furthest
much/many	more	most

tall   famous   hot   busy   interesting   friendly   old   thin

Comparative   **Superlative**

1 _____   _____

2 _____   _____

3 _____   _____

4 _____   _____

5 _____   _____

6 _____   _____

7 _____   _____

8 _____   _____

1 4 ▷ Read the sentences about Manchester and underline the correct form of the adjectives.

1 Manchester is in the north of England and is the UK's fifth **largest / larger** city.

2 Manchester has **most / more** students than any other city in the world.

3 Manchester's Chetham's Library is the **old / oldest** public library in the English-speaking world.

4 **Many / More** languages are spoken in Manchester than any other city in Western Europe.

5 The world's **first / last** passenger train station was built in Manchester in 1830.

6 Recently, Manchester was voted the **better / best** UK city to live in.

7 Manchester airport is **larger / largest** than Birmingham airport.

8 Manchester United is the **more / most** successful football club in England with 20 league titles.

9 Manchester Piccadilly is one of the **busy / busiest** train stations in England.

10 **More / Most** than 20 Nobel prize winners have come from Manchester.

1 5 ▷ In pairs, discuss the facts you read in Exercise 14. What information did you already know? What did you find interesting or surprising?

1 6 ▷ Write some sentences about a city you know. Include comparative and superlative adjectives. Use the internet to help you find information.

1 7 ▷ Work in groups and read your sentences to each other. Say which information is the most interesting and which is the most surprising.

TIP 1 7

In exam speaking tasks, show you know the vocabulary and grammar connected with the topic. Try not to give very short answers. Let the examiner see what you know.

SPEAKING: TALKING ABOUT TRANSPORT AND TOWNS

18▷ **You are going to talk together in pairs. Read and do the task.**

- Work in pairs.
- Student A, ask student B the questions about transport.
- Student B, ask student A the questions about his/her hometown.
- Use as much vocabulary as you can remember from the unit to answer the questions.
- Use comparative and superlative adjectives.
- Then swap questions.

Transport

1 How did you travel here today?
2 How do people prefer to travel in your country?
3 Is traffic a problem in your town?
4 Is it better to walk or cycle where you live?
5 What is the best way to travel in your town?

Your hometown

1 Where do you come from?
2 Tell me about the most interesting places in your town.
3 What is the oldest part of your town?
4 Is your town popular with tourists?
5 How could you make your town better?

19▷ **Now, read some questions about your answers to Exercise 18. In pairs, discuss the questions together.**

1 What vocabulary from the lesson did you use in your answers?
2 Are there any words you forgot to use?
3 Did you use comparative and superlative adjectives in your answers?
4 Did you give any short answers? How could you make your answers longer?

WRITING: A LONGER PIECE OF CONTINUOUS WRITING

20▷ **Read the task.**

This is part of an email you receive from an English pen-friend, Sandy.

I'm coming to your country next month on holiday. Where do you think I should go and why are those places interesting? What's the best way for me to travel around?

- Now write a letter, answering Sandy's questions.
- Write your letter in about **100** words.

21▷ **Before you write your email, plan your answer. Make notes on each question Sandy asks. Think about the vocabulary and grammar you can use.**

22▷ **Now, write your email.**

You can begin like this:

Hi Sandy,

I'm really pleased you're coming to visit my country. The first place you should visit is….

> **Useful linkers to include**
> if   so   because   after that

23▷ **Compare your email with your partner. Help each other to correct any mistakes with comparative and superlative adjectives and check spelling and punctuation. Give each other suggestions on how to improve your emails.**

GRAMMAR AND VOCABULARY

01 ▶ **Match the activities with the places.**

You might go here to

1	send a parcel.	A	supermarket
2	stay for a few days.	B	police station
3	speak to a policeman.	C	library
4	exercise.	D	station
5	have a meal.	E	sports centre
6	do some food shopping.	F	post office
7	catch a bus or a train.	G	hotel
8	relax on the grass.	H	park
9	borrow a book.	I	museum
10	look at things from the past.	J	restaurant

02 ▶ **Match the places in the box to the sets of words.**

department store	castle	airport	motorway	train	street	cafe

1	_____	seat	ticket	platform	travel
2	_____	lift	floor	clothes	toys
3	_____	cars	road	sign	fast
4	_____	coffee	snack	talk	table
5	_____	houses	cars	bikes	neighbours
6	_____	history	visitors	building	museum
7	_____	flight	plane	passenger	pilot

03 ▶ **Look at the map and complete the sentences using words in the box.**

next	in front of	on your left	behind
on your right	across	opposite	between

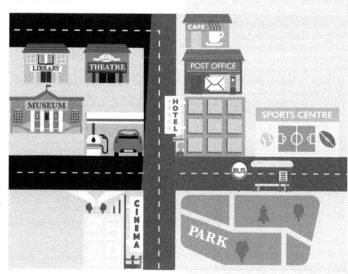

1 The park is _____ the cinema.
2 The petrol station is _____ the road from the cinema.
3 The post office is _____ the cafe and the hotel.
4 The theatre is _____ the petrol station.
5 The sports centre is _____ to the hotel.
6 When you come out of the hotel, the post office is _____ .
7 The bus stop is _____ the park.
8 When you come out of the museum, the library is _____ .

04 ▶ **Read the sentences and underline the correct answer.**

Sally and her friend had nothing to do and they felt a bit **1 bored / sorry / heavy**. They decided to go to the shopping centre to get some **2 latest / new / early** clothes. The shopping centre had all of Sally's **3 popular / favourite / great** shops. It was the weekend, and the centre was **4 full / busy / crowded** of people. Sally was **5 worried / ready / careful** not to spend too much money. After a couple of hours, Sally and her friend felt **6 wrong / difficult / tired** so they went to a cafe to relax. They had a drink and a **7 right / healthy / fast** snack and then went home.

05 ▶ **Complete the sentences using the adjectives in the box.**

friendly   high   comfortable   old   famous   interesting   modern

1 I didn't enjoy the flight because my seat was not at all _____ .
2 The library looks very _____ – the building is made of glass and it is an unusual shape.
3 The staff at the hotel were always polite and _____ .
4 I'm reading a very _____ book at the moment about the future of the planet.
5 I bought some beautiful _____ jewellery from the market. It's from the 19th century.
6 The mountain isn't very _____ but the views from the top are still amazing.
7 I sat next to a well known actor on the train. I had never seen a _____ person before that.

06 ▶ **Complete the table using the adjectives in the box.**

expensive   interesting   modern   comfortable   strong   fast   difficult low   high   careful   new   important   cheap   crowded   clean   old

+er / est	more / the most …
small – smaller, smallest	famous – more, the most famous

07 ▶ **Complete the sentences using the adjectives in brackets.**

1 I think trains are _____ (**safe**) and _____ (**fast**) than cars.
2 The traffic is usually _____ (**bad**) in the city than in the countryside.
3 In London, the bus is _____ (**cheap**) than the trains.
4 The main square is _____ (**old**) than any other parts of the town.
5 My old house was _____ (**big**) than the one I live in now.
6 I live far from college so I have to get up _____ (**early**) than my friends.
7 Our garden always looks _____ (**pretty**) in summer than in winter.
8 My friend has lost weight and is much _____ (**thin**) than last year.
9 It is _____ (**good**) for your health to cycle to work than get the bus.
10 Jon lives _____ (**far**) away from me than Pete.

0 8 ▶ **Complete the sentences using a comparative adjective.**

1 My bike was expensive but my brother's was _____ .

2 Art galleries are interesting but museums are _____ .

3 Madrid is hot but Kuwait is _____ .

4 This garden is pretty but the one we saw yesterday was _____ .

5 This restaurant is good but the Italian one is _____ .

6 I was excited about the trip but my friend was _____ .

7 Cars are noisy but motorbikes are _____ .

8 I'm bad at maths but my friend is _____ .

0 9 ▶ **Look at the pictures of the three cars. Complete the sentences using the superlative adjectives.**

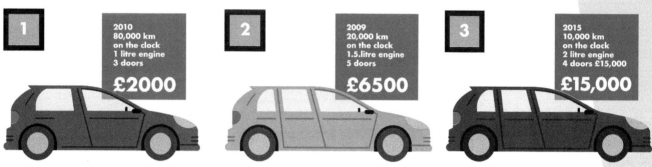

2010
80,000 km
on the clock
1 litre engine
3 doors
£2000

2009
20,000 km
on the clock
1.5.litre engine
5 doors
£6500

2015
10,000 km
on the clock
2 litre engine
4 doors £15,000
£15,000

1 Car A is _____ (**cheap**).

2 Car B has _____ (**many**) doors.

3 Car C has _____ (**large**) engine.

4 Car A has _____ (**many**) kilometres on the clock.

5 Car C is _____ (**expensive**).

6 Car A has _____ (**small**) engine.

7 Car B is _____ (**old**).

1 0 ▶ **Complete the email using the correct form of the adjectives in brackets.**

Reply Forward

To: Sue
From: William

Hi Sue,

I'm on holiday in Munich and I'm having a great time. We are staying in a little hotel near the city centre. It isn't **1** _____ (**good**) hotel in town but it is nice enough and it was **2** _____ (**cheap**) than most of the others I looked at. It's very close to the Englischer Garten, a beautiful park that is **3** _____ (**big**) than Central Park in New York!

Yesterday, we went to the Deutsches Museum, a big science museum – one of **4** _____ (**large**) in Europe. I liked all of it, but **5** _____ (**interesting**) part for me was the space exhibition. Tomorrow, we are going to the Residezmuseum. The guidebook says it is one of **6** _____ (**fine**) palaces in the whole of Germany. I can't wait.

Write and tell me about your holiday.

William

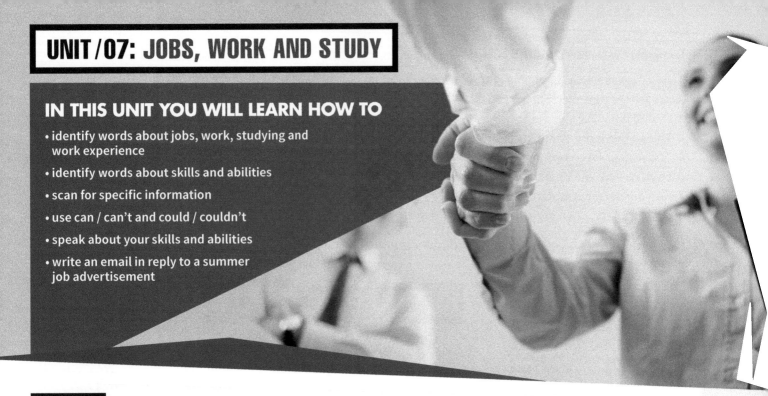

UNIT /07: JOBS, WORK AND STUDY

IN THIS UNIT YOU WILL LEARN HOW TO

- identify words about jobs, work, studying and work experience
- identify words about skills and abilities
- scan for specific information
- use can / can't and could / couldn't
- speak about your skills and abilities
- write an email in reply to a summer job advertisement

LEAD-IN

01▶ Look at the photos. What are the people doing? Write A–D in the boxes.

| **A** helping the elderly | **B** wearing a uniform | **C** meeting | **D** studying |

VOCABULARY: SKILLS AND ABILITIES

02▶ Read and match the skills and abilities A–J with the pictures, 1–10.

> A write well   B talk to new people easily   C read a map   D play sport well
> E cook many types of food   F work for long hours   G understand maths easily
> H speak many languages   I remember a lot of information   J do well in exams

TIP 02

Skills and abilities are very similar. They both talk about what you are able to do. Skills are things you learn but abilities could be things you learn or are already able to do. In this unit, we will look at them as being the same idea.

03▶ In pairs, talk about what skills from the word box in Exercise 2 you are good at and which ones you are not good at.

LISTENING: NOTE COMPLETION EXTENSION

04▶ You are going to listen to a radio advertisement about a TV programme called *Before They Were Famous*. In pairs, read the notes once quickly. Think about what information could be missing.

TIP 04

As you read through the notes, try to predict which information could be missing. Then, when you listen, you will already know what type of information to listen out for. Information could include:

numbers: dates, times, years, ages
words: nouns, names, adjectives
Note that if the answer is a number, you can avoid spelling mistakes by writing the figure and not the word, e.g. you could write *4* and not *four*.

Before They Were Famous: Jack Riley, famous **1** _____

TV Programme details

Day: **2** _____

Channel: **3** _____   Time: **4** _____

Jack's life before he was famous

left school at the age of **5** _____ .

failed exams in both **6** _____ and **7** _____ .

got a job in an **8** _____ restaurant near his home.

trained to be a chef in **9** _____ .

Jack's life now

has presented a radio show called **10** _____ since 2006.

wrote his first bestselling cookbook in **11** _____ .

worked as head chef at *The Lemon Grove* between **12** _____ and

13 _____ .

married with **14** _____ children.

05▶ Now, listen to the radio programme and complete the notes.

06▶ Listen again to the radio advertisement in Exercise 5. In pairs, talk about what TV chef Jack Riley could and couldn't do in the past and what he can and can't do now.

🎵 13

07▶ Now, complete the table with TV chef Jack's abilities in the box.

| understand maths easily   write well   write books   do well in exams |
| cook only one type of food   cook many types of food   work long hours |

	Present	Past
Able to	*can* 1 _____ 2 _____ _____	*could* 3 _____ _____
Not able to	*can't* 4 _____ _____	*couldn't* 5 _____ _____ 6 _____ _____ 7 _____ _____

08▶ Read the Grammar box. Then, complete the dialogue using *can / can't / could / couldn't*.

Present Ability	Past ability
We use *can* to talk about what we are able to do now. We use *can't* or *cannot* when we want to say that we are not able to do something. **Questions** *Can you read a map?* *What sports can you play?*	We use *could* to talk about what were able to do in the past We use *couldn't* or *could not* when we want to say that we were not able to do something in the past. **Questions** *Could you read a map?* *What sports could you play?*

A Tell me about what you think your skills and abilities are.

B Well, I have a good memory. I **1** _____ remember lots of information, which is really useful when I'm studying for my exams.

A That's really helpful. How about sport? Are you good at it?

B No, not really. I **2** _____ really play sport that well. When I was younger, I **3** _____ play badminton a little bit, but I stopped because I found it boring.

A What skills do you want to learn?

B I'd like to be better at making friends. When I was a child, I **4** _____ talk to new people at all. I'm a little better now, but I'm still quite shy. Other skills I'd like to improve on are my cooking skills. In the past, I **5** _____ cook anything very well without burning it, but I've been taking cooking classes and I **6** _____ cook many different types of food, like curry, risotto and sweet and sour chicken. My next challenge is to learn how to make sushi – I love Japanese food!

SPEAKING: DESCRIBING SKILLS AND ABILITIES

09 ▶ Look at the questions about skills and abilities. Write down three more questions about skills and abilities.

 Think about the grammar you will use, including *can / can't / could / couldn't.*

Skills and abilities questionnaire
1 What are your best skills and abilities?
2 What skills do you want to learn?
3 What skills and abilities did you have when you were younger?
4 What skills and abilities did you **NOT** have when you were younger?

10 ▶ You are going to speak about your skills and abilities, and ask and answer the questions in Exercise 9. Before you speak, spend one minute preparing what you could say and make notes.

◉ Try to add more information about your answer and don't give short answers. You can give reasons or examples. Use *because* for reasons and *for example / like* for examples.

11 ▶ Now, in small groups, ask and answer the questions in Exercise 9. As you speak, write down the other students' answers.

Questions	Student 1	Student 2
1 What are your best skills and abilities?		
2 What skills do you want to learn?		
3 What skills and abilities did you have when you were younger?		
4 What skills did you **NOT** have when you were younger?		

VOCABULARY: WORK EXPERIENCE

12 ▶ Match the summer jobs in the box to photos 1–5.

| lifeguard   sales assistant   sports coach   video game designer   helping elderly people |

13▶ Read the introduction to a factual text about summer jobs. Then, in pairs, answer the questions.

SUMMER JOBS

Helen Green is a careers advisor who works with teenagers and young adults. In this article, she explains how young people can use their summer holidays to get some work experience.

1 What do you think a career advisor does?
2 What will she do in this article?

14▶ Now, take two minutes only to read the article once quickly. Then, answer the questions.

1 Why is it good for young people to get a summer job or do a short course?
2 How many different types of summer jobs does Helen Green write about?

TIP 14

Reading the text quickly (or 'skimming' the text) will help you to understand the main ideas.

BE A **SPORTS COACH** AT A SUMMER CAMP

Can you play football, basketball or tennis? Are you good at teaching people new skills? Then this could be the job for you. Working as a sports coach allows you to spend time outside, play the sports you love and get paid for it! It will give you useful experience of working with young people, which is ideal if you are thinking of doing a teaching course in the future.

HELP **ELDERLY PEOPLE** IN YOUR TOWN

Working with elderly people is a really good way of helping others while giving something back to the community. You will help elderly people who can't go to the supermarket, so having a car would be very useful. However, if you don't there are a lot of other things that you can do. You can help them use computers, clean their homes, do the gardening and simply be there to keep them company. Contact your local care home to find out about opportunities for summer work.

WORK IN FASHION

How about working in a designer clothes store during your summer holiday? There are plenty of opportunities to use a variety of skills. You can use your fashion knowledge to help people choose the right outfit or use your knowledge of technology to show people how the latest designer smart watch works. This type of job is often very sociable as sales assistants will need to speak to customers and with other members of staff. It is a good opportunity to work as part of a team.

BE A LIFEGUARD AT YOUR LOCAL SWIMMING POOL

Being a lifeguard is an excellent choice if you want to become more confident and develop your decision-making skills. To get a job as a lifeguard, you need to take a swimming test and get a certificate. You also need to do a short training course. In the summer months, local swimming pools are often busier and are open for longer, so there will be a lot of lifeguard jobs available, but you might have to work long hours on some days of the week.

LEARN TO BE A DIGITAL DESIGNER

Are you interested in computers and learning how to design computer games? You probably won't be able to find a job in an IT company, but many of them have training programmes for young people during the summer holidays where they can learn a wide range of IT skills.

This is a great choice for anyone who is thinking of studying a computer-related course at university. These courses and jobs are very popular these days, so it will definitely be useful to get some experience!

15▶ First, read the question. Then, read the Exam strategy box about answering *True / False / Not Given* questions.

TIP 15
> If the exact information in the statement is not mentioned in the text about the statement, then the answer is **Not Given**.

1 Helen Green thinks that it is difficult for young people to find a summer job.

A True   **B** False   **C** Not Given

Answer: B (She says it's not the case at all.)

> ### Exam Strategy: answering **True**, **False** or **Not Given** questions
> **1** Read the statement very carefully.
> **2** Highlight the key words in the statement.
> *Helen Green thinks that it is difficult for young people to find a summer job.*
> **3** Find the paragraph in the text with the information about this statement.
> **Getting a summer job**
> A summer job will give you the chance to earn money and get some work experience, as well as learn new skills. Many teenagers think that it will be difficult to find a job because they don't have as much experience as an adult. However, that's not the case at all.
> **4** Scan the text for the key words you highlighted in the statement. Watch out for 'synonyms' (different words with the same meaning),
> e.g. *young people = teenagers.*
> **5** Use the exam strategy information to decide whether the statements are **True**, **False** or **Not Given**.

16▶ Now, read the article in Exercise 14 again and use the exam strategies in Exercise 15 to answer the questions. Choose the correct answer, A, B or C.

1 Young people should give employers information about what they can do.
   A True   **B** False   **C** Not Given

2 Sports coaches at a summer camp don't get paid very much money.
   A True   **B** False   **C** Not Given

3 You need to have a car to get a job working with older people.
   A True   **B** False   **C** Not Given

4 Young people who work in designer clothes stores can help customers decide what to buy.
   A True   **B** False   **C** Not Given

5 Sales assistants in designer fashion stores shouldn't talk to other staff members at work.
   A True   **B** False   **C** Not Given

6 You only need to get a certificate, to get as job as a lifeguard.
   A True   **B** False   **C** Not Given

7 In the summertime, lifeguards often need to work in the evenings or at the weekend.
   A True   **B** False   **C** Not Given

8 Many IT companies offer jobs to young people in the summer.
   A True   **B** False   **C** Not Given

WRITING: AN EMAIL FOR A SUMMER JOB

17▶ Read an email you received with an advertisement about summer jobs. In pairs, read the task and discuss what you could write in your email.

If you are interested in applying for one of our summer jobs, fill in an application form with your details and which job you want to do, and send it to me Simon Stone, summer job co-ordinator.

In your application, you should:
- say which job you are interested in.
- say what skills and abilities you have.
- say what skills you didn't have in the past but you do have now.

Write your email in about 60–80 words.

18▶ Now, look at a student's email replying to the summer jobs advertisement. What job does she want to do?

> **To:** Simon
> **From:** Laura
>
> Dear Simon,
>
> I'm interested in the hotel receptionist job. I think I have good skills to be a hotel receptionist.
>
> I could talk to new people easily and I could speak three languages – English, Spanish and Arabic. I can't work long hours but I want to learn this.
>
> I have a lot of experience. When I was younger, I worked in a restaurant.
>
> Thanks,
>
> Laura

19▶ Now, read Laura's email again in Exercise 18. In the table, tick ✓ the features she uses in her email.

Feature	✓
She says which job she is interested in.	
She says what skills she has.	
She says what skills she didn't have in the past but does now.	
She uses a good structure – greeting to start the email and ends with her name.	
She uses the correct and appropriate grammar.	
She **only** talks about the information in the instructions.	
She uses the correct number of words.	

20▶ Now, you will write an email to Simon Stone. You can choose any of the summer jobs from Exercise 14. In your email, you should:

- use a greeting to start and a polite ending – to help the reader, you can use separate paragraphs for some of the separate points in the instructions.
- write the correct number of words (60–80).
- write about all parts in the instructions – **DO NOT** add anything extra.
- check your writing for mistakes – think about how you use **can** / **can't** / **could** / **couldn't**.

 21▶ Write your email from Exercise 17, replying to Simon Stone.

22▶ In pairs, compare your emails from Exercise 21. Complete the table and give advice to each other about how you can improve your emails.

Feature	✓ ?
He/She says which job he/she is interested in.	
He/She says what skills he/she has.	
He/She says what skills he/she didn't have in the past but does have now.	
He/She uses a good structure – he/she starts with a greeting and ends with his/her name	
He/She uses correct and appropriate grammar.	
He/She **only** talks about the information in the instructions.	
He/She uses the correct number of words.	

01▶ **Match the two halves of the sentence.**

1 John works many hours, but he doesn't mind because he

2 Julia learnt Spanish very quickly this year. I think it is because she

3 I have improved a lot. I got top marks for my essay, but just a year ago, I

4 Jim's results are really impressive and he didn't even study that much. He

5 In the job interview, it's important that you don't forget anything.

6 Matteo will become a chef one day, I think. He

7 Sandra is very popular and has so many friends. It's difficult to believe that she

8 I know it is simple but I need to use my calculator because I

9 Joseph is really good at football, tennis and basketball.

10 Lucy is late. I think she is lost. She

A can cook many types of food.

B could already speak two other languages.

C can't understand maths very easily.

D couldn't even talk to new people easily a few months ago.

E Can you remember a lot of information?

F can finish early on Fridays.

G couldn't even write very well.

H Could he play sport well when he was a child, too?

I can't read maps very well.

J can just do very well in exams.

02▶ **Complete the sentences using the correct form of the verbs in the box.**

| get | learn(x2) | teach | pass | start (x2) |
| fail | take(x2) | finish | study | |

1 I _____ my driving test last month. Now, I drive to school every day.

2 My older sister is _____ law. When she _____ university, she wants to be a family lawyer.

3 I think that it is difficult for young people to _____ a good job without experience.

4 My father _____ me how to cook when I was a child.

5 I didn't _____ how to play a musical instrument when I was younger. I would like to _____ piano lessons, but they are very expensive.

6 Many students _____ the exam. They will _____ it again next month.

7 I _____ my computer course last week. I want to _____ how to design my own website.

8 My friend is _____ her new job tomorrow. She feels a bit nervous.

03▶ Match the jobs in the box with the pictures.

| waiter | chef | lifeguard | shop assistant | receptionist | teacher | cleaner | doctor |

1 _____

2 _____

3 _____

4 _____

5 _____

6 _____

7 _____

8 _____

04▶ Complete the missing information in the jobs advertisement using the words in the box.

| experience | friendly and helpful | sports, art or music | energy |
| long hours | speak another language | hard-working | weekend |

SUMMER JOBS FOR STUDENTS

Waiter/Waitress needed for popular Italian restaurant. You do not need to have **1** _____ of working in a restaurant, but you should be **2** _____ and happy to work in a team. You will work **3** _____, especially at the weekends when we are very busy.

Receptionist for busy city hotel, who can **4** _____ (French, German or Spanish). You should be **5** _____ to guests and tell them any information that they need about tourist attractions, local restaurants and transport in the city.

Summer Camp Leaders to teach children **6** _____ at a summer camp. You should have a lot of **7** _____ because you will spend all day with the children. You will need to work weekdays and at the **8** _____, but you will have one day off each week.

05▷ Complete the sentences with the prepositions, *in / on / at*.

1 My brother is working as a lifeguard _____ the swimming pool.
2 My cousin studies nursing _____ university.
3 I wouldn't like to work _____ a restaurant. I think it would be too stressful.
4 I'm not working _____ Monday. It is my day off.
5 My friend wants to be a chef _____ a top restaurant.
6 I was _____ work yesterday, so I didn't watch the football match on TV.
7 I usually finish work _____ five o'clock.

06▷ Complete the categories with the correct words from the box.

| waiter   receptionist   tables   rooms   chef   guests   cash desk |
| clothes   meal   lift   cleaner   changing rooms   shop assistant |

Restaurant	Hotel	Shop

07▷ Read the conversation and underline the correct option.

A 1 **You can / You can't / Can you** play sport?
B Yes, 2 **I can / I can't / can I** play basketball. Are you good at sport?
A Not really, 3 **I can / I can't / can I** play many sports, but I like watching them on TV.
B How many languages 4 **you can / you can't / can you** speak?
A Four. 5 **I can / I can't / can I** speak English, Russian, Chinese and Thai.

08▷ Complete the sentences using *can / can't / could / couldn't*.

1 I'm doing well at school. I got top marks for my English essay. I think it's because
I _____ write really well.
2 I got a bad mark in my exams. My problem is that I _____ remember facts.
3 I was nervous last year in my science exam that I _____ remember a thing.
4 I did really badly in my history exam last summer. I didn't do enough homework so
I _____ understand the subject very well.

09▷ Read the email and decide if the use of *can / can't / could / couldn't* is correct ✓ or incorrect ✗. Correct the mistakes.

Dear Simon,
I'm interested in the lifeguard job this summer.
1 I **could** swim very well. 2 I **couldn't** swim when I was a child but I learnt when I was 12.
3 I **can** also remember lots of information and instructions very well.
I have some questions about the lifeguards you had last year. 4 They **could** talk to new people easily? 5 I **can** so I think I am a good choice for this job.
Thanks,
Pablo

1 _____   2 _____   3 _____
4 _____   5 _____

IN THIS UNIT YOU WILL LEARN HOW TO

- identify speaker's attitudes and feelings
- recognise distractions
- identify health activities and ways to relax
- understand a writer's views
- use modals *should* / *shouldn't* and *have to* / *don't have to*
- answer multiple-choice questions
- describe a picture
- write an email in reply to a friend to give advice

LEAD-IN

0 1 ▶ Look at the pictures. In pairs, ask and answer the questions.

- What sport do you play?
- How do you like to keep healthy?
- Are there any activities you enjoy / don't enjoy doing? Why / Why not?

LISTENING 1: MATCHING

0 2 ▶ You are going to listen to Part 1 of a conversation between three friends, Samantha, Tom and Sarah. The first voice you will hear is Samantha. Listen to the first part of the conversation and answer the questions.

1 Where does Tom plan to go? _____

2 What is Sarah thinking of doing? _____

03 ▶ Now, listen to Part 2 of the conversation. Find and underline the key words in each opinion. Then, tick ✓ the person, Samantha, Tom or Sarah, who gave the opinion.

TIP 03

Identify key words in each sentence. The sentences are listed in the same order as in the conversation in the Listening.

Example: <u>Joining</u> the <u>gym</u> is <u>too expensive</u>.

Opinion	Samantha	Tom	Sarah
1 Joining the gym is too expensive.			
2 Running is a boring way to exercise.			
3 It is more fun to exercise with other people.			
4 It is better to exercise outdoors.			
5 It is a good idea to pay for a personal trainer.			
6 It is important to follow a healthy diet.			

VOCABULARY AND SPEAKING

04 ▶ Match the activity words in the box with the pictures.

> play tennis   go cycling   watch TV   play basketball   drink water
> enjoy art and music   eat fruit and vegetables   get enough sleep

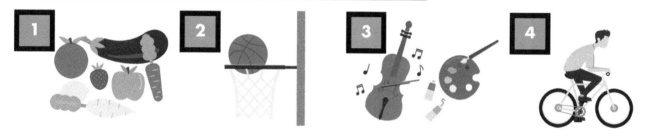

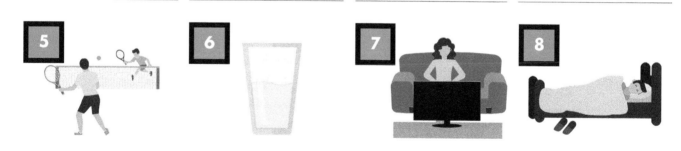

05 ▶ In pairs, read and discuss the following questions.

1 Do you do any of these activities in Exercise 4? How often do you do them?
2 Do you think these activities in Exercise 4 are healthy? Why / Why not?
3 Imagine you have some important exams at school. You are working very hard and are feeling quite stressed and tired. Which of the activities would be a good way to help with stress? Why?

06 ▸ You are going to read an essay about the importance of exercising while studying for exams. Take two minutes to scan the essay very quickly. Which of the activities from Exercise 4 does the essay talk about?

TIP 06

The skills of skimming and scanning are important when reading a text. First skim a text quickly to understand the main idea. Then, read the text again at normal speed, scanning, looking for particular information and details.

Essay question: *Students who are studying for important school exams should stop sports lessons. Discuss.*

Some parents may think that while their children are preparing for important school exams, they shouldn't have sports lessons. This could be because they want them to focus on exam subjects more, like science and maths. For a similar reason, some parents think children should also stop painting and music lessons in the final school term so they can spend more time studying. However, I disagree with these views, and believe that children should continue to have sports lessons. These lessons help students keep healthy and happy during the exam period.

Firstly, schools need to encourage young people to follow a healthy lifestyle and get regular exercise. Many young people don't do enough exercise. They prefer to spend their free time indoors on their computers or watching TV than going to the park and playing tennis, or going cycling.

Many people today are overweight and have health problems. There is a lot of information about eating healthily, but people often forget that regular exercise is equally important. Secondly, exercise helps us feel less stressed and tired. It also improves memory and helps us think clearly. When students are studying for exams, it's a good idea to take regular breaks and do something active for 20 minutes. Exercise also helps us to concentrate better on difficult tasks and helps us sleep better at night. Doing exercise may even help students get better results in their exams.

In conclusion, I believe that students who are revising for important exams should continue to have sports lessons because regular exercise is good for their body and mind.

07 ▸ Read the text in Exercise 6 again and answer the questions.

1 Does the writer of the essay agree or disagree with the essay question?
2 What opinion does the writer give in response to the essay question?

08 ▷ Now, look at the question and read the exam strategy.

1 The writer believes that children who have important exams

   A need sports lessons to keep healthy.

   B don't need to focus on other subjects.

   C need to spend all their time studying.

> **Exam strategy: answering multiple-choice questions**
>
> 1 Read the statement very carefully.
>
> 2 Highlight key words in the question and multiple-choice options.
>
> > 1 The writer thinks that children who have important exams
> > A need sports lessons to keep healthy.
> > B don't need to focus on exam subjects more.
> > C need to spend more time studying.
>
> 3 Find the paragraph in the text with the information about this statement.
>
> 4 Highlight information in the text related to the multiple-choice options.
>
> *Some parents may think that while their children are preparing for important school exams, they shouldn't have sports lessons. This could be because they want them to focus on exam subjects more, like science and maths. For a similar reason, some parents think children should also stop painting and music lessons in the final school term so they can spend more time studying. However, I disagree with these views, and believe that children should continue to have sports lessons. These lessons help students keep healthy and happy during the exam period.*
>
> 5 Choose which of the answer options is correct.
>
> **Answer:** A

TIP 08

In some Reading exams, you will need to answer multiple-choice questions. There is only one correct answer option and the other two are distractors. Read the question and answer options, then read the text again to find which answer option matches the information in the text exactly.

09 ▷ Read the essay again and use the exam strategy to answer the multiple-choice questions. Choose the best option, A, B or C.

1 The writer says many young people prefer to spend their free time

   A riding their bikes.

   B in the park.

   C in front of their computers.

2 The writer thinks that exercise for young people is

   A less important than diet.

   B just as important as diet.

   C more important than diet.

3 The writer believes regular exercise can make people feel

   A more active.

   B less stressed.

   C more tired at night.

4 The writer thinks that exercising

   A benefits the body and the mind.

   B can affect studying in a negative way.

   C will help you get better exam results.

10 ▶ Read the statements using *should* and *shouldn't / should not*. Then, underline the correct option in sentences 1–3.

Children **shouldn't** have sports lessons.

Children **should** have more lessons in their exam subjects, particularly science and maths.

Children **should not** attend painting and music lessons.

1 The writer thinks it is a **good / bad** idea for children to have sports lessons.

2 The writer **wants / doesn't want** children to have more lessons in their exam subjects.

3 The writer's advice for children is **to go / not to go** to painting and music lessons.

11 ▶ Read the Grammar box and check your answers.

should	shouldn't / should not
We use *should* when we want to show that:	We use *shouldn't / should not* when we want to show that:
• something is a good idea. • we want something to happen. • we want to give advice for something.	• something is a bad idea. • we don't want something to happen. • we want to give advice against something.

Should and *shouldn't / should not* are modal verbs and so <u>never change form</u> in the present tense.

We use a verb in the infinitive form, such as *do* or *make* <u>after</u> **should** and **shouldn't / should not**.

We can use **should** in questions to ask for someone's advice.

***Should** children have sports lessons in school?*

Note the incorrect word order: *Children should have sports lessons in school?*

12 ▶ Read the sentences and underline the correct answers.

1 You **should / shouldn't** eat lots of fruits and vegetables. It is really good for your health.

2 Don't watch TV all day. You **should / shouldn't** only watch around three hours a day.

3 We **should / shouldn't** sit all day without doing some type of exercise.

4 I think we **should / shouldn't** all sleep between seven to 10 hours every night.

5 My friend **should / shouldn't** spend all day on a computer and play more sport instead.

13 ▶ You are going to describe a picture. First, look at the picture and read the sentences. Then, put the sentences A–C in the correct order.

A <u>I think</u> the boy **should** go to sleep <u>because</u> he is tired and it is bed time. He **shouldn't** play on his computer for so long. <u>I think</u> he **should** play more sport.

B <u>I think</u> the boy <u>is playing</u> on his computer at night. <u>It looks like</u> the boy is tired.

C <u>The picture shows</u> a boy in his bedroom. <u>There is</u> a computer, a lamp and a bed.

1 4 ▶ Now, look at the pictures and read the instructions. You should:

- talk generally about what you can see.
- give specific details about the pictures.
- give your opinion and reasons.
- use words and language related to health.
- give advice using *should / shouldn't*.
- talk for 1–2 minutes.

TIP 1 4

When you are describing a picture, you can use these words and phrases.

When starting a sentence: *This picture shows …, In this picture, I can see …, There is / are …*

Being more specific: *It looks like …, I think* + present continuous … For example, *I think the boy is playing.*

Giving your opinion and reason: *I think … because …, He / She / It / They should / shouldn't …*

VOCABULARY: HOW TO RELAX

1 5 ▶ Match the ways to relax in the box with the pictures.

| drink tea   do yoga   go for a walk   do exercise   read a book |

16▶ You are going to listen to five people talk about their favourite way to relax. Listen and match the speakers with the activities from Exercise 15.

16

1 Jim _____

2 Elena _____

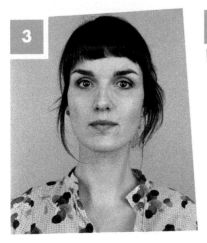

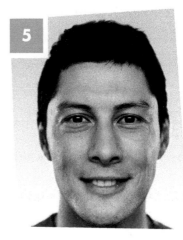

3 Kate _____

4 Mike _____

5 Mark _____

17▶ Listen again and choose the correct answer, A, B or C.

16

1 Jim thinks that people who feel sad shouldn't

  A forget about their problems.

  B read a funny book.

  C read a sad book.

2 Elena thinks that if you want to do yoga, you should

  A do it at your own home.

  B find the right teacher.

  C not pay lots of money.

3 According to Kate, a common reason for not doing regular exercise is

  A it takes too much time.

  B it is too expensive.

  C it will make a person tired.

4 How much time does Mike usually spend outside on his lunch break?

  A 20 minutes

  B 30 minutes

  C 60 minutes

5 Which does Mark do to help him relax?

  A He drinks some green tea.

  B He has a cup of tea before bed.

  C He tries to get enough sleep.

TIP 17

Look carefully at the first part of the question. The speaker may mention details that are similar to all three answer options, but only one option matches the information exactly.

18 ▷ Read the Grammar box. Then, read the sentences and underline the correct answer.

have to	*don't have to*
We use *have to*: • for rules and laws. • to show that there is a need or obligation to do something. *Have to* changes to *has to* for *he / she / it*.	We use *don't have to*: • to show there is a choice. • to show there is **NOT** a need or obligation. *Don't have to* changes to *doesn't have to* for *he / she / it*.

We use a verb in the infinitive form, such as *do* or *make* <u>after</u> *have to / don't have to*.

We can use *have to* in questions to ask if there is a choice or an obligation to do something.

Do you have to wear school uniform?

1 We **have to / don't have to** arrive to school on time. It's one of the school's rules.

2 The deadline for our homework isn't until next week, so we **have to / don't have to** do it tonight.

3 **You have to / Do you have to** play sport at school?

4 He didn't go to school yesterday, so he **have to / has to** give the teacher a doctor's note.

5 We **don't have to / doesn't have to** study languages but my teacher recommends it.

19 ▷ Look at the task and read the email. Then, answer the question.

Your friend Alice has asked her friends for advice about being healthy. Another friend, Helen, has replied to her email.

To: Alice
From: Helen

Hi Alice,

I think it's a good idea to play tennis or basketball. Playing sport is a good way to stay healthy. I don't think you should play computer games all day. You should make sure you get enough sleep every night, between seven and 10 hours. You don't have to study for hours and should try to take regular breaks. You should eat lots of fruit and vegetables and get lots of regular exercise.

Being healthy gives you more energy and makes you feel good.

From,

Helen

1 What activities does Helen say are a good idea?

20 ▷ Use the information you learnt in this unit to write an email in reply to your friend Alice. In you email, you should:

• say what activities Alice can do to stay healthy.

• include types of healthy activities and ways to relax.

• say why it is important to stay healthy.

• use should / shouldn't / should not / have to / don't have to / do not have to.

• write 80–100 words.

21 ▷ In pairs, compare your emails. What vocabulary and grammar does your partner use? How can you improve your partner's email?

GRAMMAR AND VOCABULARY

01 ▶ Match the different sporting activities in the box with the pictures.

| play basketball | do yoga | do exercise |
| play tennis | go for a walk | go cycling |

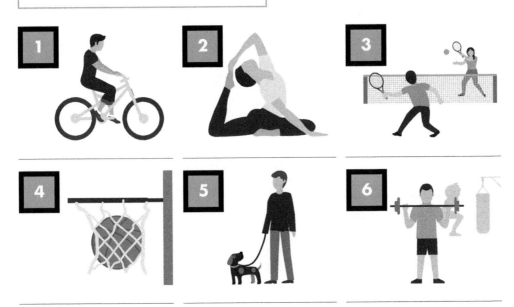

02 ▶ Complete the sentences using the correct form of the verbs in the box.

| get(x3) | drink(x2) | do(x2) | eat | have | join | go(x2) | play(x2) |

1 It can be expensive to _____ a gym, but they often have a lot of modern equipment.

2 It is very important to _____ plenty of water whenever you _____ exercise.

3 I _____ lots of fruit and vegetables and _____ yoga twice a week.

4 I like to _____ running in the park so I can _____ some fresh air when I exercise.

5 It is a good idea to _____ a personal trainer to _____ advice about living healthily.

6 I _____ tennis three times a week and _____ for walks in the park.

7 It is important to _____ lots of sleep every night.

8 When you _____ green tea, it can help you relax.

9 Many young people _____ a sport or do exercise at school.

03 ▷ Read the dialogues and decide if the sentences are correct ✓ or incorrect ✗. Then correct the mistakes.

1 A What you should eat to be healthy?

B It is important to eat lots of fruit and vegetables.

☐ _____

2 A Is it important to exercise?

B Yes, you should exercise for at least 150 minutes a week.

☐ _____

3 A Is it a good idea to play computer games for many hours?

B No, you should play on your computer for so long.

☐ _____

4 A Do you have any other advice about being healthy?

B I think you should find ways to relax.

☐ _____

5 A What is the best way to relax?

B I like doing yoga. I think you shouldn't try it.

☐ _____

04 ▷ Complete the conversation using *should / shouldn't / should not* and a verb in the box.

| eat | drink | play | ride | watch | get |

A Did you see that programme last night about how to stay healthy? I learnt so much.

B Really? I didn't see it. Did you think it was interesting?

A Yes, it had lots of useful suggestions. Do you know we **1** _____ five glasses of water a day? I never normally have that much but I'll try from now on.

B That's a good idea. I always think I **2** _____ more sleep. Did it mention anything about sleep?

A Yes, it said we should sleep for at least eight hours. However it's not always possible.

B I only sleep for about seven hours, so I think I should go to bed earlier.

A Yes, it will give you more energy. The other thing it warned against was watching too much TV. It said we **3** _____ more than two to three hours a day.

B Did it mention what activities are good for you?

A Well, any exercise is good. You **4** _____ sport at school if you like it. If not, you **5** _____ a bicycle or walk to school instead of going by bus or car.

B What about food? Did it give any advice about healthy eating?

A Yes, and I think this was the most important piece of advice. We **6** _____ fast food more than once a week and make sure we eat at least five pieces of fruit and vegetables a day.

05 ▶ **Read the sentences and underline the correct answer.**

1 We **have to** / **don't have to** wear sports clothes during sport lessons otherwise we can't take part.

2 You **have to** / **don't have to** pass a swimming test to be a lifeguard at the swimming pool.

3 You **have to** / **don't have to** be fit to do yoga because anyone can try it.

4 You **have to** / **don't have to** spend a lot of money to stay healthy. You can go running in the park for free.

5 We **have to** / **don't have to** wear special shoes when we play football. Otherwise, it is difficult to run.

6 You **have to** / **don't have to** join the gym to take exercise classes, but they cost less for members.

7 Professional sports players **have to** / **don't have to** practise for at least three hours a day.

8 You **have to** / **don't have to** be good at sports to stay fit, but regular physical activity is good for you.

06 ▶ **Complete the texts using** *has to* / *have to* / *doesn't have to* / *don't have to*.

1 At school, there are some new rules. The most important one is that we _____ turn off our mobile phones before the lesson. However, unlike most schools, we _____ wear school uniform every day. We can wear our own clothes.

2 At university, students can come to classes whatever time they want. They _____ come into class every morning. It is their choice. However, the university has a special rule about students who can't attend due to illness. If they are going to be late, they _____ send an email to their teacher.

07 ▶ **Complete the dialogue using** *should* / *shouldn't* / *should not*.

A I enjoy playing tennis but I want to improve. What **1** _____ I do?

B My advice is you **2** _____ practise as much as possible. How often do you play?

A Twice a week at the moment. Is that enough?

B No, I suggest you **3** _____ train more often. I don't think it's possible to improve if you don't play more.

A I know I **4** _____ have rest days when I don't practise. Do you think I need to play every day then? Is it really necessary?

B Maybe not every day, but you **5** _____ just play twice a week – that's not enough. That's my advice. Also, it's a good idea to get help from someone who can teach you. I think you **6** _____ have tennis lessons.

08 ▶ **Match the two halves of the sentences.**

1 It is a good idea to pay   A great way to keep fit.

2 Joining the gym   B a healthy diet.

3 It is more fun when you go   C for a personal trainer.

4 It is important to follow   D running with other people.

5 I think it's better to do   E can be expensive.

6 Running is a   F yoga than go to the gym.

IN THIS UNIT YOU WILL LEARN HOW TO

- identify words used to communicate with other people
- use *going to* and adverbs of time for future plans
- listen to a discussion about a language project
- give a long talk about a topic
- use collocations
- skim read to understand the main idea in an article
- write a short essay on a topic

LEAD-IN

01 Look at the pictures. Match the ways of learning English in the box with the pictures.

study with a teacher in a classroom	talk to people whose first language is English
use a dictionary	listen to songs in English
keep a vocabulary notebook	watch videos online
read newspapers and magazines	write an email to a friend

02 In pairs, discuss which ways of learning English from Exercise 1 work best for you and why.

VOCABULARY AND SPEAKING

0 3 Read the sentences and underline the correct answers.

1 Can you phone me when you are free? I need to talk **for** / **to** / **by** you.

2 When you apply for a job, I think it is best to communicate **to** / **with** / **by** email first.

3 The weather is a popular topic to discuss **for** / **about** / **by** in the UK.

4 Your parents are really friendly. Whenever I visit your home, they always chat **about** / **with** / **for** me.

5 I know enough of the language to hold a conversation **with** / **for** / **to** someone.

0 4 Match the sentence halves.

1 What is the main language that
2 Do you prefer to communicate
3 How often do you talk
4 What do you usually chat
5 Do you think reading newspapers

A can help with language learning?
B about with your friends?
C you speak in your country?
D to people on the internet?
E by phone or by email?

0 5 In pairs, ask and answer the five questions in Exercise 4.

GRAMMAR: *GOING TO* FOR FUTURE PLANS

0 6 Complete the plans using a verb in the box.

learn meet send study video call

1 I'm going to _____ my friends at the cinema tonight.

2 I'm going to _____ my cousin on the computer this afternoon. He's moving to Canada next week.

3 Whenever I read a newspaper, I say to myself: 'I'm going to _____ five new phrases today'.

4 I'm going to _____ in the library this morning.

5 I'm going to _____ an email to my English friend at the weekend.

0 7 In pairs, discuss the plans in Exercise 6 and answer the questions.

1 How do we know the writer is talking about future plans?
2 Which adverbs of time does the writer use in the sentences?

TIP 07

We use adverbs of time, such as next week, tomorrow and later, when we know the exact time of the action. We don't need to use them if we are making a general statement about a future plan or the plan is only a possibility. Adverbs of time usually go at the end of the sentence.

08 ▷ Read the Grammar box and check your answers to Exercise 6.

Present continuous *going to* for future plans

We can use present continuous *going to* to:

***tell* someone about a plan.**

person	verb *to be*	(not) *going to*	plan
I	*am*	*going to*	*learn five new phrases.*
We	*are*	*not going to*	*talk about school.*

***ask* someone about a plan.**

verb *to be*	person	*going to*	plan
Are	*you*	*going to*	*move to Canada?*
Is	*he*	*going to*	*video call his cousin later?*

ask questions with question words.

question word	verb *to be*	person	*going to*	plan
What	*are*	*you*	*going to*	*do at the weekend?*
Where	*is*	*he*	*going to*	*go to university?*

09 ▷ Read the sentences and decide whether they are correct ✓ or incorrect ✗.
Correct the mistakes.

1 When I am 18, I going to study in the UK. ☐
_____

2 Are you going to come shopping with me later? ☐
_____

3 I'm not going to order any food at the restaurant – I'm not hungry. ☐
_____

4 She is going buy a new smartphone at the weekend. ☐
_____

5 You are going to tell your parents that you got bad results on your science exam? ☐
_____

6 Where are you going to watch the football match, at home or at your uncle's house? ☐
_____

10 ▷ In pairs, talk about your future plans. Discuss what you are going to do and when.

TIP 10

In everyday speech, people may pronounce *going to* as *gonna*. Generally, *gonna* is acceptable in informal spoken language **BUT** you shouldn't ever use *gonna* in formal or written English.

LISTENING: DISCUSSING A LANGUAGE PROJECT

11 ▷ You are going to hear two students, Sofia and Oliver, at an international college discussing what they are going to do for a language project. Read the questions and listen to their conversation. Then, decide whether these sentences are *True* or *False*.

1 There are over 200 students in the school who speak more than one language.   True / False

2 Oliver thinks that they shouldn't only include numbers in the report.   True / False

3 Oliver can speak more than one language.   True / False

1 2 ▷ Listen again and complete the table with the correct information. Then, answer the question.

Name	Room where they work
Miss Wainwright	1 _____
Miss Smith	2 _____
Mr Black	3 _____

4 Where is Sofia going to next?
A The library.
B The maths classroom.
C The cafe.

SPEAKING: A LONGER TALK ABOUT A TOPIC

1 3 ▷ **You are going to talk for one to two minutes about a topic. First, read the task and make notes about what you could say.**

Describe a language that you are studying, other than your first language. You should say:

- what the language is.
- how well you know the language.
- how long you are going to study the language for.

Now explain why you are learning this language.

In some Speaking exams, you will be asked to talk about a topic. The topic is a personal experience. You will be given one minute to prepare your talk and make notes. You can use your notes in the talk to help you.

1 4 ▷ **In pairs, do the task. Ask and answer follow-up questions about the topic.**

VOCABULARY AND READING

1 5 ▷ **Complete the collocations with the correct verb, A, B or C.**

1 _____ a conversation
A speak   B do   C hold

2 _____ an advantage
A make   B have   C do

3 _____ your skills
A have   B get   C practise

4 _____ an effort
A make   B give   C take

5 _____ some work
A practise   B do   C hold

6 _____ fun
A get   B begin   C have

7 _____ a language
A get   B hold   C speak

8 _____ someone's advice
A do   B take   C speak

9 _____ time (to do something)
A have   B practise   C do

10 _____ progress
A do   B make   C have

TIP 1 5

A collocation is a word or a phrase that sounds natural and correct when it is used with another word or phrase. Collocations are not part of grammar but they make use of grammar. We prefer to say:

Before my holiday, I'm going to have extra English lessons. (NOT: take extra English lessons.)

Can you take care of your brother this afternoon? (NOT: have care)

I'm going to have a cup of tea. (NOT: take a cup of tea.)

1 6 You are going to read an article about a teenager who has a special skill. Skim the article once quickly and answer the questions.

1 Who is Richard Doner?
2 What is special about him?

MULTILINGUAL:
WHAT IT IS LIKE TO SPEAK MANY LANGUAGES

1 Today, over 50% of the world's total population can speak more than one language. Maybe you are one of these people who can communicate in many languages. However, it may be unlikely that you can speak more than Richard Doner, an American teenager who can hold a conversation in over twenty languages.

2 Richard lives in New York. It is a city where there are people from hundreds of different countries. There are around 180 languages spoken in New York schools. This is why Richard believes that New York is the perfect city for him. 'I can discuss many different topics with people from all over the world and I don't even need to travel to another country,' Richard says.

3 Can he see a disadvantage? 'You can never rest. You have to continuously practise and put in lots of effort all the time to be able to remember the languages. I believe that, if your brain doesn't do any work, you can forget what you know. I don't have time to speak all of my languages every day, so if I want to get better, if I want to make progress, the important thing is that I speak each one as often as I can. If I don't, I start to forget the phrases and words that I know'.

4 He also believes that when you learn a language, you don't only learn words or phrases. 'A language helps you begin to learn more about the people and their cultures – their ideas, their food, what is important to them and so on'.

5 Richard is very popular all over the world. There are lots of videos online of him practising his skills in a wide range of languages, such as Arabic, Mandarin, German and even Swahili – a language that is common in West Africa.

6 The most important thing for Richard is to have fun when he learns a language. Learning is easier if you can make it interesting for yourself, he explains. 'Also, take your time – you have to learn at a speed that works for you'. I don't think many would disagree with him!

1 7 Read the first three paragraphs again and underline the correct words to summarise the main ideas.

1 Richard Doner is very special because he can speak **more** / **less** / **most** languages than **more** / **most of** / **most** people.
2 Richard is very lucky as he has **many** / **any** / **lots of** opportunities to practise his language skills.
3 Richard practises speaking each language **all the time** / **regularly** / **every day** to improve.

TIP 1 7

Most paragraphs have one main idea. This helps the reader to understand what the writer wants to say. When you read a paragraph, it is always a good idea to think about what the main idea is, and try to summarise it in fewer words.

18 Now, read paragraphs 4, 5 and 6 in Exercise 16 again and summarise the main ideas in one sentence.

1 _____

2 _____

3 _____

READING: SENTENCE COMPLETION

19 Read paragraph 2 from the article in Exercise 16 again.

Richard lives in New York. It is a city where there are people from hundreds of different countries. There are around 180 languages spoken in New York schools. This is why Richard believes that New York is the perfect city for him. 'I can discuss many different topics with people from all over the world and I don't even need to travel to another country,' says Richard.

20 Read some sentences about the article in Exercise 16. Then, complete the sentences using NO MORE THAN THREE words.

1 In New York City, you can find people from a large number of _____ . (Paragraph 1)

> Question sentence:
> In New York City, you can find people from a large number of _____ .
> Article sentence:
> It is a city where there are people from hundreds of different countries.
> **Answer:** *different countries*

2 If Richard wants to talk with people from different countries, it isn't necessary to travel _____ . (Paragraph 2)

3 To remember languages, Richard makes sure his brain does _____ . (Paragraph 3)

4 If you know a language, you can start to understand about the people and _____ . (Paragraph 4)

5 Swahili is a popular language in _____ . (Paragraph 5)

6 When he learns a language, it is absolutely necessary for Richard to _____ . (Paragraph 6)

TIP 20

In some exam questions, you will be asked to complete a sentence using no more than three words. You need to paraphrase the original sentence from the article and write only the set number of words. Remember you will lose marks for writing more than the specified number of words.

WRITING: SHORT ESSAY ON A TOPIC

21 In pairs or small groups, discuss the questions.

1 What type of information do you find in a dictionary?

2 Do you prefer to use a paper dictionary or a dictionary on the internet? Why?

22 In your pairs or groups, read the essay question. Then, make notes about how you could answer the question.

What are the advantages and disadvantages of using an online dictionary in a language class?

Example: *It is easy and quick to look up a word that you don't know.*

2 3 Read the names of four parts of an essay. Organise the parts in the correct order.

A Paragraph (disadvantages)

B Conclusion

C Introduction

D Paragraph (advantages)

2 4 Read a student's essay answering the question in Exercise 22. Don't worry about the gaps for now.

Many students use an online dictionary to help them learn a language when they study in class. In this essay, I **1** _____ discuss the advantages and disadvantages of this.

Firstly, if a student doesn't **2** _____ the meaning of a word or phrase, they can find it quickly and easily with an online dictionary. The teacher can continue with the class and doesn't need to stop and answer questions all the time. **Furthermore**, a paper dictionary is sometimes too heavy and students don't like to carry one in their bags.

On the other hand, when a student is not very confident, or if they are afraid of **3** _____ a mistake, they might start to use their dictionary in the wrong way. If they stop to **4** _____ every word or phrase they do not know, they won't **5** _____ their language skills enough and they won't improve. **Additionally**, it is very difficult for a teacher to check that the students are **6** _____ their computers to look **7** _____ a word and not just playing online games. If they do not focus on the class, they won't **8** _____ any progress.

To sum up, an online dictionary is often useful for students. **However**, in my opinion, students should only go online when the teacher says to do so. If not, they won't learn for themselves.

2 5 Read the student's essay again in Exercise 24 and choose the best answer, A, B or C.

1 A am going   B going to   C am going to

2 A see   B know   C think

3 A having   B doing   C making

4 A look   B see   C check

5 A practise   B try   C speak

6 A using   B use   C used

7 A up   B at   C to

8 A do   B make   C have

2 6 Now, look at the words in bold in the essay that the student uses to organise ideas. Complete the table using the words or phrases in bold.

In the essay, decide which words or phrases introduce:		
The main idea of a paragraph at the start of the essay	1	_____
		_____
Extra information about an idea	2	_____
	3	_____
A new, different idea	4	_____
	5	_____
The conclusion	6	_____

2 7 ▶ Use the information from this unit to write an essay about a topic. The topic of your essay is:

What are the advantages and disadvantages of taking English lessons with classmates from the same country?

In your essay, you should include:
- a clear introduction and conclusion, and main paragraphs discussing the topic.
- words and phrases to organise ideas.
- advantages and disadvantages.

You should write 220–250 words.

MODEL ANSWER

Many students are interested in learning English. Some students can go to English speaking countries and learn with other students from all over the world. Most students though study in their own country and have to learn with people who have the same first language as they do. I would like to discuss the advantages and disadvantages of this.

Firstly, if a student doesn't know the meaning of a word or understand the teacher they can ask one of their classmates for help. Secondly, the teacher will understand what problems the class have with learning English and be able to help them with the things that they find most difficult.

On the other hand, if a student is shy or just lazy they can speak their own language in the lesson all of the time and not communicate in English. If they ask their friends for help too often, they won't improve their skills.

To sum up, it can be helpful for students if they can get help from friends who speak the same language as they do. If the whole class speaks the same first language, he or she can help them with difficult grammar and vocabulary. However, if a student is in a class where everybody has the same first language they have to be very motivated to be successful.

GRAMMAR AND VOCABULARY

01 Complete the sentences using a preposition or adverb. Not all sentences need a preposition or adverb.

1 I usually communicate _____ email with my lecturer at university.
2 If you are having a difficult time, it is best to talk _____ someone.
3 You must be able to hold a conversation _____ someone to pass the exam.
4 You can't take the course, unless you speak _____ English really well.
5 Have you got any free time? I want to have a chat _____ something.
6 You can go to the careers office to have a chat _____ someone about jobs.
7 Do you want to discuss _____ a topic for the project?

02 Match the sentence halves.

1 I'm going to study   A to songs in English.
2 I'm going to talk   B with a teacher in a classroom.
3 I'm going to use   C newspapers and magazines.
4 I'm going to listen   D to people whose first language is English.
5 I'm going to keep   E emails to my friends.
6 I'm going to watch   F a vocabulary notebook.
7 I'm going to read   G online videos.
8 I'm going to write   H a dictionary.

03 Complete the sentences and questions using the positive, negative or question form of *going to* for future plans and the verbs in brackets.

0 ___I'm going to buy___ (+ / buy) a paper dictionary as I can't use an online dictionary in class.
1 _____ (– / worry) about my English test tomorrow. It is only a practice exam.
2 _____ (? / you / learn) some French before your holiday in Paris?
3 _____ (+ / try) my hardest to improve my vocabulary over the next few weeks.
4 _____ (? / you / meet) them outside the library?
5 _____ (– / she / live) in campus accommodation when she goes to university.

0 4 ▷ Write questions using *going to* for future plans and the words below.

0 what / going to / do / after lunch / ?

What are you going to do after lunch?

I'm going to cycle home and do my English homework.

1 who / going to / do / language project with / ?

_____

Probably Peter, but if he already has someone to work with, I'm going to ask Aaron.

2 where / going to / buy / a dictionary from / ?

_____

There is a big book store near my house. I'm going to go there.

3 how / going to / improve / your language skills / ?

_____

Practise, practise, and more practise.

4 when / going to / tell / teacher you want to move up to a higher class / ?

_____

I don't know. Maybe I should do it after the next lesson.

5 why / not going to / go to university next year / ?

_____

I am going to work for my father's company instead.

0 5 ▷ Complete the conversation using the words in the box.

time	advantage	skills	advice	effort	progress	fun	work

Susan My brother says he won't be able to pass his English exam, so he's not going to make an **1** _____ .

George Well, that's not a surprise. He never does any **2** _____ .

Susan I tried to give him some **3** _____ , but he didn't take it. He only wants to have **4** _____ , he doesn't care about studying.

George I did, too. I told him that it takes a long **5** _____ to learn a language, and it's hard work.

Susan He watches films in English and does look up what the actors are saying on the internet.

George That's a good start. He should also practise his speaking **6** _____ as well as listening.

Susan Exactly. It's more difficult to make any **7** _____ if you don't speak.

George He also has a big **8** _____ because your dad is an English teacher! Maybe you can encourage him to try more.

0 6 ▷ Complete the paraphrased sentences of the conversation in Exercise 5. Write ONE and THREE words only.

1 Susan's brother isn't going to study because he believes he is going to fail _____ .

2 He didn't want to take Susan's _____ .

3 Susan's brother isn't interested in his studies and he would much rather _____ .

4 George told Susan's brother that it takes a lot of effort to learn a language, and it happens over a _____ .

5 Geroge thinks that without practising your speaking skills, it is more difficult to

_____ .

6 The biggest advantage that Susan's brother has is that their father teaches _____ .

07 Complete the table using the second part of the collocations in the box.

| a mistake   dinner   a difference   a noise   an exam |
| somebody laugh   a test   a picture   a guess   a walk |

make	**take**

08 Read the sentences and underline the correct answer.

1 It is a beautiful day. I **am going to take** / **am taking** / **am going to make** a walk.

2 Lucinda is upset. She thinks she **took** / **made** / **makes** many mistakes in the exam.

3 Robert is so funny. He really **makes** / **takes** / **is making** me laugh.

4 I always **make** / **am taking** / **take** lots of photos when I go sightseeing on holiday.

5 What really **makes** / **is making** / **made** a difference to your language skills is if you don't worry about **doing** / **taking** / **making** mistakes.

09 Rearrange the linking words and phrases in the correct place in the paragraph.

I'm going to talk about a project I did at college. **1 To sum up,** it was a language project, and I worked with my friend, Peter. We had to find out how many people in college speak more than one language and, **2 firstly**, what their level of English is. I like doing this sort of project, so was happy to work hard. **3 However**, Peter is also a very good student, so we helped each other a lot, and it was quite easy in the end. **4 Furthermore**, we didn't get any good advice from Miss Smith in the college office. She didn't want to do anything for us at first. Then she gave us the information from last year, not this year, and then she couldn't find the correct information herself! **5 Additionally**, she didn't help us at all.

1 _____   2 _____   3 _____

4 _____   5 _____

10 Complete the sentences using the correct form of the verbs in the box.

| have (x2)   discuss   hold   communicate   try |

1 I don't know what university to apply for. My father and I _____ a chat about it tomorrow.

2 Come in, Alison. We _____ to decide what to have for dinner, maybe you can help us.

3 Look, we _____ this last week – I don't want to have a party for my birthday.

4 I don't know anyone who _____ by letter anymore. I only ever send emails.

5 Our English teacher always tells us _____ more conversations with each other after class, so we can practise our skills more.

6 I _____ a chat with my mum about what language course to take.

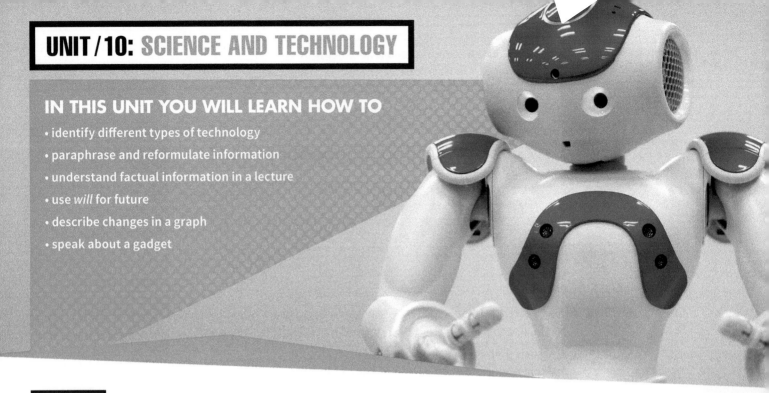

UNIT / 10: SCIENCE AND TECHNOLOGY

IN THIS UNIT YOU WILL LEARN HOW TO

- identify different types of technology
- paraphrase and reformulate information
- understand factual information in a lecture
- use *will* for future
- describe changes in a graph
- speak about a gadget

LEAD-IN

01 ▷ Match the technology words in the box with the pictures.

desktop computer   laptop   smartphone   letter
tablet   landline telephone   smart TV   smart watch

1

2

3

4

5

6

7

8

02 ▷ In pairs, discuss when you use the types of technology in Exercise 1. Ask and answer the questions.

Which one(s) do you use for:
- studying?
- contacting friends?
- searching the internet?

> *I use my smartphone to contact my friends. I can call or message them.*

VOCABULARY AND READING

0 3 ▷ **Read the sentences and underline the correct spellings.**

1 My computer **crushed** / **crashed** / **crached** and I lost my homework.
2 You need to **shout down** / **shot down** / **shut down** your laptop when you finish using it.
3 There are some excellent **wepsites** / **websites** / **websides** that can help you to study.
4 I own three **devices** / **advices** / **divises** – a smartphone, a laptop and a tablet.
5 The computers at school are all connected to the same
   netwalk / **netwok** / **network**.

TIP 0 3
It is important that you spell words correctly in exams, otherwise you will lose marks.

0 4 ▷ **Complete the sentences using the correct words in the box.**

attachments	backup	download	store	stream

1 If you don't know who sent you the email, then it isn't a good idea to open the _____ .
2 I often _____ music from the internet.
3 You can _____ films online a few months after they are released at the cinema.
4 You should create a _____ of your files, so you don't lose them.
5 The *cloud* is the name for the place on the internet where you can _____ your files.

0 5 ▷ **You are going to read an article about the internet. Skim the article once quickly. What is the best title for the article, A, B or C.**

A New developments on the internet
B How people communicate on the internet ·
C Why people use the internet

1 The internet is still quite a new development in technology, however it is impossible to think about life without it. It works in a very simple way. It takes information and sends it from one computer to another. It is not a difficult job, but it is a very big one. There are hundreds of millions of computers connected to the internet at the same time. However, they don't all do the same thing. Some computers are like a digital box that store information, (like videos or music files) that people see, read or listen to. These stores of information are called servers, and there are three categories.

2 The first type is a file server, which holds ordinary documents. The second is a mail server for sending and receiving emails. The third is a web server for web pages. We know these servers store information but how do people find this information or send it to each other? For this, you need a client.

3 A client is a computer that gets information from a server and delivers it to another computer. When you go online on your smartphone, you are using it as a client. When two computers on the internet exchange information, they are known as peers.

4 Peer-to-peer (P2P) communication is when you send someone a photo on your smartphone. When that person sees this photo, your smartphone is working as the server. It stores the photo and the other person's device is the client, which searches for your information. It then displays the photo on the other person's screen.

0 6 ▶ Read the article again in Exercise 5. Then, look at the information from the article and complete the paraphrased sentences using ONE to THREE words.

Example:

0 Paragraph 1: *It takes information and sends it from one computer to another. It is not a difficult job, but it is a very big one.*

Sending information from one computer to another is <u>an easy job</u>.

1 Paragraph 1: *There are hundreds of millions of computers connected to the internet at the same time. However, they don't all do the same thing.*

All the computers connected to the internet are doing _____ at the same time.

2 Paragraph 2: *The second is a mail server for sending and receiving emails.*

You can send and receive emails _____ server.

3 Paragraph 3: *A client is a computer that gets information from a server and delivers it to another computer.*

The client _____ from one computer to another using a server.

4 Paragraph 3: *When you go online on your smartphone, you are using it as a client.*

Your smartphone becomes the client when you use it _____ .

5 Paragraph 4: *When that person sees this photo, your smartphone is working as the server. It stores the photo and the other person's device is the client, which searches for your information.*

The client finds the photo by _____ from the server, which stores it.

◎ In some exam questions, you will need to complete a sentence using one to three words. The sentence you need to complete rewrites the information from the text in different words. This is called paraphrasing. Paraphrasing is reading something, thinking about its meanings and putting it in your own words.

TIP 0 6

Paraphrasing is important as you will need to understand it in Reading, Listening, Speaking and Writing exams.

06.0 MINI TIP The opposite of difficult is easy. The sentences use different words but they mean the same.

06.1 MINI TIP What is the opposite of the 'same'?

LISTENING 1: A LECTURE

0 7 ▶ You are going to listen to a short lecture about smartphones. Before you listen, look at the diagram. Reorder the letters in brackets to complete the parts of a smartphone.

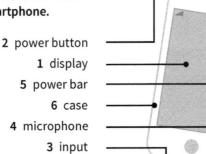

2 power button
1 display
5 power bar
6 case
4 microphone
3 input

Parts of a smartphone	Reason for these parts
1 touch screen or d__ __ __ __ __ __ (S L P I Y A)	**1** To _____ .
2 p__ __ __ __ b__ __ __ __ __ (R E W O / T O T N U)	**2** To turn the phone _____ .
3 USB i__ __ __ __ (T U P N)	**3** To _____ or to _____ .
4 m__ __ __ __ __ __ __ __ (R E N O P I C H O)	**4** To _____ when you phone someone.
5 p__ __ __ __ b__ __ (W O R E / R A)	**5** To _____
6 c__ __ __ (S A E)	**6** To _____

08.2 MINI TIP You need three words here to say both of the things it does.

08.2 MINI TIP You need to be careful with spelling. You will get the answer wrong if you spell the word incorrectly.

08▷ Now, listen to Part 1 of the lecture. Complete the second column in the table with reasons why a smartphone has each part using TWO to THREE words.

09▷ Listen to Part 2 of the lecture and complete the table.

Year	% of population with smartphones
2010	1
2015	2
2020	3
2025	4

GRAMMAR AND VOCABULARY

10▷ In Listening 1, the lecturer talked about what he thinks is definite or probable in the future. Listen again to Part 2 in Exercise 9 and complete the tables.

	Person / Thing	*will, will not / won't*	Verb (infinitive without *to*)	
For positive statements	1 _____	2 _____	3 _____	richer than they are now.
For negative statements	4 _____	5 _____	6 _____	the same as the one in the picture today.

	will, will not / won't	Person / Thing	Verb (infinitive without *to*)	
For questions	7 _____	8 _____	9 _____	the same as they do now?

	Question word	*will, will not / won't*	Person / Thing	Verb (infinitive without *to*)	
Or	10 _____	11 _____	12 _____	13 _____	like?

11▷ Read part of a student's end-of-year school report. Do you think he will be happy with it?

END-OF-YEAR
SCHOOL REPORT

Michael Brown

Michael's result in maths improved. His score was 74% at the start of the year and increased to 82% by the end of the year. His English grade also went up from a C to an A, so this was very good. However, his science result fell by 6%, from 92% to 86%. There was also a decrease in his business score (78% to 72%). Hopefully, these will rise again next year.

12 ▶ Look again at the school report. Michael's teacher has used different words to describe changes. Complete the information in the chart using the words in the school report.

TIP 1 2

The vocabulary in blue and red is useful when you want to describe changes, especially when numbers get bigger or smaller. Use a dictionary to check words you are unsure about.

Verb (infinitive)	Verb (past)	Noun
1 _____	2 _____	a rise
3 _____	increased	4 _____
5 _____	went up	–
6 _____	fell	7 _____
8 _____	9 _____	a decrease
to go down	10 _____	–

13 ▶ Look again at the information in the table in Exercise 9. Draw a line on the axis below to show the percentage (%) increase of the population with a smartphone between 2010 and 2025.

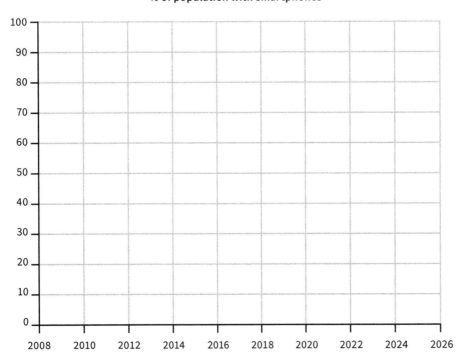

% of population with smartphones

14 ▶ Now, read the short description and choose the correct answer, A, B or C.

The percentage of people with smartphones **0** __A__ **1** _____ 38% in 2010 **2** _____ 62% in 2015. In the future, this **3** _____ will **4** _____. At the end of the period in 2025, this percentage will **5** _____ on 86%.

0 A increased   **B** increase   **C** increasing   **Answer:** A

1 A at   **B** from   **C** to

2 A to   **B** by   **C** at

3 A rised   **B** rose   **C** rise

4 A to continue   **B** continue   **C** continuing

5 A finish   **B** finishing   **C** be finish

15▷ Look at the line graph and use the language in Exercise 12 to describe the way each line in the graph changes.

1 Smartphone: _____

2 Laptop: _____

3 Smart watch: _____

4 Tablet: _____

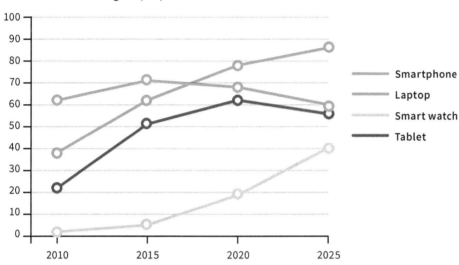

Percentage of people who own the devices from 2010 to 2025.

16▷ In pairs, compare your answers to Exercise 15.

LISTENING 2 AND GRAMMAR

17▷ You are going to listen to a student, Lorenzo, answer a question about technology. Read the question and listen to Lorenzo's answers.

Describe a piece of technology that you would like to buy in the future.

18▷ Look again at Lorenzo's answers and the underlined words in the listening script. Then, match the underlined words in Lorenzo's answers with the definitions.

1 Important and interesting parts of a device. _____

2 The newest device you can buy. _____

3 To move your finger from one side to the other on a device. _____

4 A device that is old. _____

5 The part of a device that stores data. _____

19▷ Listen again and match the questions with Lorenzo's answers. Write 1–4 next to the questions. There are two extra questions.

A How will it make your life better? _____

B How much does it cost? _____

C Where do you want to buy it from? _____

D What does it look like? _____

E Why do you want to buy it? _____

F Why is it so popular? _____

20 ▷ In pairs, you are going to talk about the same topic as Lorenzo in Exercise 17. Choose four of the questions in Exercise 19 that you could answer. Then, complete the sentences.

Describe a piece of technology that you would like to buy in the future.

1 You should say _____

2 And you should say _____

3 You also need to say _____

4 And don't forget to tell me _____

21 ▷ Now, in pairs, swap your books with your choice of questions. You are going to answer your partner's questions. You have two minutes to prepare what you are going to say.

22 ▷ When you are ready, decide who is going to go first. You each have one minute to give your talk about the piece of technology you have chosen.

GRAMMAR AND VOCABULARY

0 1 ▶ Read the sentences and underline the correct answer.

1 My brother **streams** / **stores** his files on his computer but doesn't back them up.
2 You can connect a series of computers together on a **website** / **network**.
3 I prefer to use a **laptop** / **desktop** computer as I can work from anywhere.
4 Stop playing games! **Shut down** / **Crash** your computer right now!
5 I don't like paying a lot of money for **attachments** / **apps**, but it can cause problems if you only **download** / **backup** them for free.

0 2 ▶ Complete the sentences using the words in the box.

stream	website	device	crash	attachment	backup

1 A set of pages of information on the internet about a particular subject. _____
2 A copy of the files from your computer that you keep in a different place. _____
3 A machine, like a smartphone, that can connect to the internet. _____
4 A file, like an essay, that you add to an email before sending it. _____
5 This happens when your computer suddenly stops working. _____
6 Music or video that you watch on the internet without downloading it first.

_____

0 3 ▶ Complete the interview using the words.

A How **0** ___will people travel___ (people / travel) around in the future?

B In cars that don't have anybody driving.

A Isn't that dangerous?

B No, the cars **1** _____ (communicate) with each other and make sure they all have enough space on the road.

A That's amazing!

B Yes, it is. There **2** _____ (are not) any crashes ever again.

A **3** _____ (the cars / able to) to fly?

B Maybe – I can certainly imagine a mix of a car and an aeroplane.

A And food – what **4** _____ (people / eat)?

B Similar meals to the ones we eat today, but with a lot less meat.

A Why is that?

B Well, in the future, if we want to continue to eat as much meat as we do now, we
5 _____ (definitely need) more space for animals than we actually have on the planet.

A I see. Maybe we could build farms on the moon?

B Hmmm … I'm not sure that **6** _____ (be) possible.

A Why not? It's a great idea!

B Well, how **7** _____ (the animals / breathe) when they are on the moon?

0 4 ▷ Look at the graph and read the sentences. Describe which part of this graph does each sentence refer to? There are extra sentences.

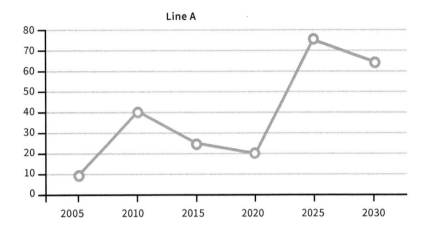

Line A

1 It increased from 10% to 40%. _____

2 This rise will continue after 2025. _____

3 It decreased by 15%. _____

4 It fell by 30%. _____

5 It will finish on 65%. _____

6 It went up from 40% to 50%. _____

7 It will fall again after 2020. _____

8 There will be a rise of 55%. _____

9 It went down by 5%. _____

10 There was an increase of 35%. _____

0 5 ▷ Complete the description of the changes to Line B in the graph using the words in the box.

| fall   down   rise   decrease   went   increased   2020   55%   50%   2015   40%   2005 |

After it **1** _____ from 30% in
2 _____ to **3** _____ in
2010, line B **4** _____ up by another
20% between 2010 and 2015. This was its highest
point. It started to **5** _____ in 2015,
going **6** _____ to 40% in
7 _____ . It will **8** _____
to 50% in 2025, and then will **9** _____
to 45% in 2030.

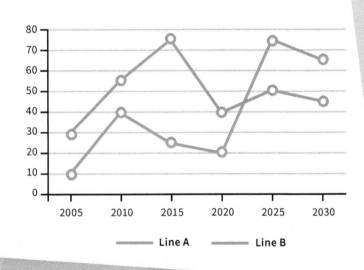

Line A   Line B

06 ▷ Which is the best summary A, B or C for this graph in Exercise 5?

A Both lines went up and down a lot. Line A changed much more than Line B.

B The biggest changes for Line A will happen in the last ten years shown on the graph. However, Line B had its own most important changes earlier, especially between 2005 and 2015.

C Line A went up to 40% in 2010, then down to 20% by 2020, and then up to 75% in 2025 and back down to 65%, so there was a lot of change. Line B increased to 75% in 2015, then went down to 40% in 2020, so a lot of change there as well. It didn't change much after that, only up by 10% and then down by 5%.

07 ▷ Read an email from a grandfather to his teenage grandson and underline the correct answers.

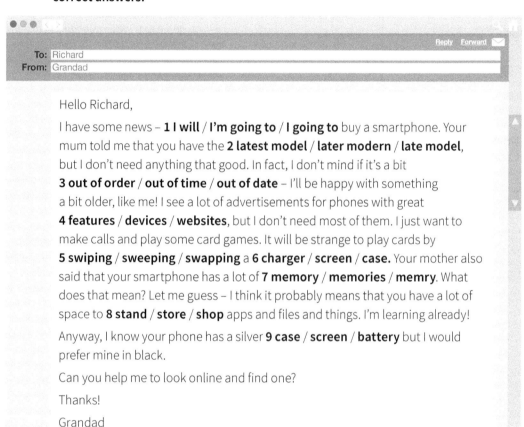

Reply Forward ✉

To: Richard
From: Grandad

Hello Richard,

I have some news – **1 I will / I'm going to / I going to** buy a smartphone. Your mum told me that you have the **2 latest model / later modern / late model**, but I don't need anything that good. In fact, I don't mind if it's a bit **3 out of order / out of time / out of date** – I'll be happy with something a bit older, like me! I see a lot of advertisements for phones with great **4 features / devices / websites**, but I don't need most of them. I just want to make calls and play some card games. It will be strange to play cards by **5 swiping / sweeping / swapping** a **6 charger / screen / case.** Your mother also said that your smartphone has a lot of **7 memory / memories / memry**. What does that mean? Let me guess – I think it probably means that you have a lot of space to **8 stand / store / shop** apps and files and things. I'm learning already!

Anyway, I know your phone has a silver **9 case / screen / battery** but I would prefer mine in black.

Can you help me to look online and find one?

Thanks!

Grandad

ANSWER KEY

UNIT 1   DAILY LIFE

Lead-in
1 Possible answers: wake up, sleep, have dinner, chat online, play sport
2 Student's own answers.

Vocabulary and speaking
3 1 B 2 B 3 C 4 A 5 A
4 Student's own answers.

Reading: choose the correct answer
5 Student's own answers.
6 1 A 2 C 3 A 4 B 5 C 6 A 7 A

Grammar and speaking
7 1 B 2 C 3 A
8 Group 1 – exercise, work, play, live, come, get up, help, swim, stay, cook, listen, practise
   Group 2 – catch, watch, relax, finish, switch, teach
   Group 3 – try, study
9 Student's own answers.

Reading: sentence completion
10 1 gets up 2 has 3 eats 4 gets 5 goes 6 returns 7 makes
    8 watches 9 meets 10 go 11 studies 12 goes 13 cooks
    14 exercises 15 sees 16 falls

Writing: describing a daily routine
11 Student's own answers.

Reading: matching
12 1 C 2 D 3 F 4 B 5 A 6 E

Writing: a description
13 Student's own answers.
14 Student's own answers.

Listening: matching
15 1 F 2 F 3 T
16 Jack – Australia; Carlos – USA
17 1 F 2 D 3 C 4 E 5 A
18 Student's own answers.

Speaking: talking about your day
19 Student's own answers.
20 Student's own answers.
21 Student's own answers.

Grammar and Vocabulary Unit 1
1 1 H 2 D 3 E 4 J 5 B 6 C 7 I 8 A 9 F 10 G
2 1 have 2 brush 3 meet 4 catch 5 leave 6 go 7 watch
   8 do 9 go to 10 fall
3 make – a noise, lunch, the beds, dinner, a mess,
   do – some homework, the laundry, the shopping, the cleaning, the housework
4 1 live 2 work 3 get up 4 leave 5 have 6 walk 7 catch
   8 finish 9 meet 10 go out

5 1 washes 2 watches 3 cries 4 practises 5 goes 6 does
   7 catches 8 relaxes 9 gives 10 switches off
6 1 works 2 play 3 studies 4 come 5 wear 6 like
   7 gets up 8 have 9 makes 10 begins / finishes
7 1 My friend tidies the room.   2 I play football at the weekend.
   3 I take a sandwich to college for lunch.   4 I wake up at half past six.
   5 My brother checks his phone every five minutes.   6 I have a
   shower in the evening.   7 I try to stop studying before 9pm.
   8 I go to the dentist every six months.   9 My father does most
   of the housework.   10 I visit my family at the weekends.
8 1 work 2 start 3 opens 4 fill 5 tidy 6 clean 7 work
   8 tells 9 shouts 10 take 11 finish 12 gets 13 enjoy

UNIT 2   HOUSE AND HOME

Lead-in
1 1 bedroom 2 bathroom 3 kitchen 4 living room
2 1 basement 2 hall 3 hallway 4 study 5 attic 6 garage
   7 garden

Speaking: items in a home
3 Student A – 1 curtains 2 (table) lamp 3 television/TV 4 desk
   5 shower 6 drawers
   Student B – 1 window 2 picture(s) / poster(s) 3 blind 4 sink
   5 pillows 6 oven / cooker
4 1 curtains 2 (table) lamp 3 television/TV 4 desk 5 shower
   6 drawers
   1 window 2 poster(s) 3 blind 4 sink 5 pillows
   6 oven / cooker
5 Student's own answers.

Speaking and vocabulary
6 Student's own answers.

Listening 1: picture description
7 (Picture) 2
8 1 very comfortable 2 the garden 3 to relax 4 down the hall
   5 brushes his teeth 6 a blind

Reading: note taking
9 1 Andrew Taylor 2 Prime Location Agency 3 London
   4 andrewtaylor@uniaccom.co.uk 5 by email
10 Giorgio – 2, 4, 6 Andrew Taylor – 1, 3, 5

Grammar: simple present postive, negative and questions
11 1 am not 2 live 3 doesn't live 4 Does 5 can 6 Can / speak
    7 you want 8 does
12 1 isn't 2 Is the car 3 is 4 I don't play 5 Do you play
    6 do you play 7 I play

Listening 2: short answers
13 1 NO 2 YES 3 YES 4 YES 5 NO 6 YES 7 NO 8 NO

Reading: dialogue building and matching

14 1 A   2 A   3 C   4 B   5 A   6 A   7 C   8 B
16 1 D   2 G   3 A   4 B   5 E   6 F

Reading and grammar

17 Student's own answers.
18 1 C   2 A   3 A   4 B   5 C   6 B   7 B   8 C   9 A   10 C
19 often, sometimes, always, sometimes, sometimes, usually, always, never
20 am, go, talk, tidy, help, spend, are, forget
21 1 after   2 before
22 1 I am never late for school.   2 I never forget to do my homework.
23 Student's own answers.

Speaking: choosing accommodation

24 1 Student's own answers.
25 1 Student's own answers.

Writing: an email to a friend about accomodation

26 C
27 Hi Gavin,
  I live in private accommodation. I'm very happy with my room. My bed is very comfortable. I have a big desk for studying and I have posters on the wall. The Wi-Fi here is very fast. I am happy about that because when I'm in my bedroom, I can speak to my parents online. I can also play online games. Do you have Wi-Fi in your room? Is the food nice where you live?
  Write soon,
  Giorgio
28 Student's own answers.

Grammar and Vocabulary Unit 2

1 1 bedroom   2 bathroom   3 living room   4 garage   5 hallway
   6 garden
2 1 a fridge   2 a semi-detached house   3 some drawers
   4 a living room   5 an attic   6 a cupboard   7 a chair
   8 a university campus
3 1 C   2 E   3 G   4 A   5 H   6 B   7 D   8 F
4 attic, garden, study, basement, kitchen, television/TV, desk, shower, window, sink, blind
5 1 curtains   2 table lamp   3 posters   4 pillows   5 oven
   6 wardrobe
6 1 Is it okay to come to your house this evening?   2 Can you check that the windows are all closed before we go out?   3 Are you in the living room next to the kitchen?   4 Do you want to sit in the garden?   5 Are the apartments in the UK very different from the apartments in your country?
7 1 usually live   2 always keeps his car   3 (Correct)
   4 I don't see him very often/I don't very often see him
   5 (Correct)   6 (Correct)
8 1 He never does the washing up.   2 Can you give me some advice?   3 I always leave my house at eight o'clock in the morning.   4 What time does your alarm usually go off?   5 My cousin often comes to my house for dinner.   6 Where do you want to live in the future?   7 How many people do you live with?   8 Do you live on the university campus?

UNIT 3   HOBBIES, LEISURE AND ENTERTAINMENT

Lead-in

1 1 hiking   2 canoeing   3 cycling   4 sailing   5 climbing
   6 white water rafting
2 Student's own answers.
3 Student's own answers.

Listening: multiple choice questions

4 cycling, hiking, cooking, climbing, white water rafting, sailing
5 1 C   2 B   3 A   4 A   5 C

Grammar: present simple / present continuous

6 Present simple affirmative – We get up, I usually sleep, He looks after us, He always makes
   Present simple negative – I don't miss, My friend doesn't like
   Present continuous affirmative – I'm having, I'm staying, I'm resting, We're having, The chef is cooking
   Present continuous negative – I'm not staying
7 1 continuous   2 continuous   3 simple   4 continuous
8 1 lives, living   2 gets, getting   3 carries, carrying
   4 hopes, hoping   5 washes, washing   6 runs, running
   7 plays, playing   8 rides, riding   9 lies, lying   10 passes, passing
   11 cries, crying   12 makes, making   13 sees, seeing
   14 begins, beginning
9 1 C   2 D   3 A   4 B   5 simple   6 continuous
10 1 are you doing, you want, am/'m watching, plays, are losing
   2 am/'m waiting, arrives
   3 isn't answering, is/'s studying
   4 do you / get, walk, doesn't take, drives, is working
11 1 Why are you learning English?   2 What time do you usually get up?
   3 What are you learning about in geography at the moment?
   4 Do you play tennis?   5 What is the teacher doing now?

Reading: use of distraction

12 Student's own answers.
13 1 C   2 B   3 B   4 B   5 C   6 A   7 A
14 1 professional   2 train   3 successful   4 fit   5 advice

Speaking and vocabulary

15 1 basketball   2 basketball   3 football   4 badminton, table tennis
   5 football   6 badminton, basketball, table tennis, football, chess
   7 badminton, basketball, table tennis, football, tai chi
   8 badminton, table tennis   9 chess   10 kite flying, tai chi
   11 basketball, football   12 badminton, table tennis, kite flying, tai chi, chess   13 badminton, basketball, football, table tennis, tai chi
16 Student's own answers.
17 Student's own answers.
18 Student's own answers.
19 a person running, people doing yoga, a father walking along with his son (holding hands), a couple (a man and a woman) walking together, a person doing push-ups
20 Student's own answers.

Writing: responding to a message from a friend

21 1 (Saturday) 23rd June   2 £15   3 1:00pm   4 Child in Time
   5 (an) umbrella
22 He wants to meet up.
23 Student's own answers.
24 Student's own answers.

Grammar and Vocabulary Unit 3

1 1 tennis   2 volleyball   3 basketball   4 football   5 badminton
  6 swimming   7 skiing   8 cycling   9 sailing   10 hiking

2 play – tennis, chess, volleyball, football, badminton, hockey, table tennis, basketball
  do – karate, judo, boxing, gymnastics , taekwondo, athletics
  go – horse-riding, swimming, skiing, cycling, sailing, hiking, canoeing, fishing, bowling

3 1 win   2 beats   3 play   4 hit   5 lose   6 throwing   7 kicking
  8 catch   9 scores

4 1 popular   2 team   3 hitting   4 match   5 wear

5 1 tennis, water sports   2 athletics, team sports
  3 lose, actions used in sports   4 judo, type of competition
  5 boxing, mountain sports   6 winner, sports equipment

6 third person present simple – snows, fixes, gets, stops, invites, marries, washes, makes, offers, buys, crosses, copies, dances, swims, happens, travels
  -ing form – snowing, fixing, getting, stopping, inviting, marrying, washing, making, offering, buying, crossing, copying, dancing, swimming, happening, travelling

7 1 B   2 F   3 D   4 A   5 G   6 C   7 E

8 1 I don't know   2 I can't remember   3 I don't understand
  4 is having   5 It belongs, is reading   6 I don't want to
  7 has, is taking   8 can't hear, is having

9 1 am/'m having   2 have   3 am/'m enjoying   4 like
  5 am/'m staying   6 have/'ve got   7 work   8 am/'m looking
  9 want   10 finishes

10 1 D   2 B   3 F   4 A   5 H   6 E   7 C   8 G

UNIT 4   TRAVEL AND HOLIDAYS

Lead-in

1 1 D   2 C   3 A   4 B

Vocabulary: holiday activities

2 1 try traditional food   2 go horse riding   3 visit water parks
  4 go mountain climbing   5 go on cycling tours
  6 visit beach resorts   7 go shopping   8 see famous buildings
  9 see local attractions   10 go on day trips   11 go on cultural visits
  12 stay with host families

3 Student's own answers.

Reading: reading for specific information and detailed meaning

4 Student's own answers.

5 1 F   2 A   3 E   4 B

6 Student's own answers.

Listening: interview task

7 (Example answer C)

8 Student's own answers.

9 1 B   2 A   3 B   4 B   5 B

Speaking: adding more detail and giving reasons

10 1 C   2 A   3 D   4 B

11 1 as   2 so, because

12 Student's own answers.

Grammar: past simple and present simple

13 1 4   2 1,3   3 2,5,6

14 1 Present simple – 1, 3   2 Past simple – 2

15 1 studies   2 went   3 correct   4 thinks   5 correct   6 isn't

Writing: emails

16 1 Madrid
  2 It was a city break and the weather was cold. Normally he goes on beach holidays in warm weather.

17 1 went   2 was   3 visited   4 go   5 went   6 bought   7 was
  8 ate   9 don't try   10 did   11 tried   12 was   13 was   14 took
  15 did   16 did

18 1 ✓   2 ✓   5 ✓   6 ✓   7 ✓   9 ✓

19 Student's own answers.

Speaking: experiences

21 Student's own answers.

22 Student's own answers.

23 Student's own answers.

Grammar and Vocabulary Unit 4

1 1 an adventure holiday   2 a beach holiday   3 a city break
  4 a language exchange   5 a family holiday

2 city break – go on day trips, see local attractions, go shopping, try traditional food, see famous buildings, go on cultural visits
  adventure holiday – go mountain climbing, go horse riding, go on cycling tours, visit water parks
  beach holiday – visit beach resorts
  language exchange – stay with host families

3 1 go shopping   2 go horse-riding   3 visit local attractions
  4 visit water parks   5 go on day trips   6 stay with a host family
  7 go on a cycling tour   8 go mountain climbing   9 go on a cultural visit   10 visit a beach resort

4 1 popular   2 fun   3 natural   4 local   5 boring   6 cultural
  7 interesting   8 delicious   9 famous   10 traditional

5 1 Do you like   2 I do   3 do you usually go   4 went
  5 did you do   6 enjoy   7 we all went   8 Was it
  9 don't really like   10 wasn't

6 1 went   2 don't like   3 decided   4 enjoy   5 didn't have
  6 saw   7 are   8 learnt   9 felt   10 was   11 do you like
  12 Do you prefer

7 1 D   2 E   3 A   4 B   5 C

8 1 because   2 As   3 so   4 because   5 As

UNIT 5   FOOD

Lead-in

1 1 China   2 Saudi Arabia   3 Italy   4 United Kingdon   5 Brazil

Vocabulary and speaking

2 1 D   2 E   3 A   4 C   5 B

3 Student's own answers.

Vocabulary and reading

4 Possible answers: food stalls, famous chefs, traditional activities arts and crafts

5 food stalls, famous chefs, traditional activities, arts and crafts

6 1 C   2 B   3 A   4 A   5 B   6 C

Listening: matching

7 C

8 1 B   2 F   3 A   4 E   5 G   6 H

Vocabulary and listening

10 1 flour   2 spring onions   3 garlic   4 rice   5 pasta   6 lamb
  7 salmon   8 carrot   9 onion

11 Meat – lamb
  Vegetables – carrot, onion, spring onion, garlic
  Fish/Seafood – salmon
  Carbohydrates – rice, pasta
  Other ingredients – flour

12 Student's own answers.

13 1 chop   2 mix   3 cut   4 roll   5 fold   6 boil   7 fry

14 C

15 1 mix   2 chop   3 mix   4 chop   5 cut   6 roll   7 fold   8 boil

Grammar and speaking

16 a cabbage, some meat, onions, some salt, shrimps, some water

Countable singular – a cabbage

Countable plural – (some) shrimps, (some) oranges, (some) onions

Uncountable – (some) meat, (some) salt, (some) rice, (some) milk, (some) water

17 1 a / an, a   2 some, some   3 some, some

18 1 Countable   2 Uncountable

Speaking: eating habits

19 Possible answers: 1 How much meat do you eat each week?
2 Are there any recipes you like to cook?
3 Are there many famous chefs on TV in your country?

20 Student's own answers.

Reading: sentence completion 1

21 1 C   2 F   3 A   4 E   5 D

22 1 a   2 some   3 chop / cut   4 some   5 a   6 mix   7 cut
8 fry / cook

Writing: describing a process

23 Student's own answer.

Reading: sentence completion 2

24 1 A   2 C   3 B   4 B   5 C   6 C   7 D   8 A

Speaking: a meal you enjoy

25 Student's own answer.

Writing: food in your country

26 Student's own answer.

Grammar and Vocabulary Unit 5

1 1 duck   2 lettuce   3 lobster   4 garlic   5 salmon   6 spaghetti
7 beef   8 cauliflower

2 Meat – beef, duck
Vegetables – lettuce, carrot, garlic, cauliflower
Seafood/Fish – lobster, salmon
Carbohydrates – spaghetti

3 1 C   2 A   3 B   4 E   5 D

4 1 a   2 an   3 a   4 an   5 some   6 some   7 some   8 any
9 any   10 any   11 some   12 some   13 some

5 1 a lot of   2 a lot of   3 a lot of   4 many   5 many   6 many
7 much   8 much   9 much

6 1 C   2 A   3 C   4 A   5 B   6 A   7 B   8 B   9 C   10 C

7 1 C   2 A   3 C   4 C   5 B   6 A   7 C   8 B   9 A   10 C

8 1 D   2 F   3 A   4 C   5 E   6 B   7 G

UNIT 6   TRANSPORT AND PLACES IN TOWN

Lead-in

1 1 bridge   2 stadium   3 statue   4 castle   5 tower

2 1 Sydney Harbour Bridge, Australia
2 Bird's nest stadium, China
3 Statue of Liberty, USA
4 Neuschwanstein Castle, Germany
5 Leaning Tower of Pisa, Italy

3 Student's own answers.

Reading and vocabulary

4 Places in a city – square, car park, post office , police station, library, sports centre, restaurant , cafe, shopping centre, department store
Travel and transport – car park, motorbike, coach, platform, motorway, ticket, the underground

5 Places in a city – supermarket, park, town centre, station, museum, castle, theatre
Travel and transport – parking, bus, trains, flight, boat trip, bicycles, walk, by car

6 1 C   2 B   3 B   4 A   5 A   6 C   7 A

Listening: gap-fill

7 10 am, 6 pm, Thursday, 8 pm, Wednesday, 635, 729, £3.50, £2.00

8 1 Gadzen   2 WT3 5BX   3 Thursday   4 2/two
5 15/fifteen minutes

9 1 on the left of   2 on the right of   3 opposite   4 next to
5 between

10 1 F   2 C   3 A   4 E   5 B   6 D

11 Student's own answers.

12 Student's own answers.

Grammar: comparatives and superlatives

13 1 taller, tallest   2 more famous, the most famous
3 hotter, hottest   4 busier, busiest
5 more interesting, the most interesting   6 friendlier, friendliest
7 older, oldest   8 thinner, thinnest

14 1 largest   2 more   3 oldest   4 More   5 first   6 best   7 larger
8 most   9 busiest   10 More

15 Student's own answers.

16 Student's own answers.

17 Student's own answers.

Speaking: talking about transport and towns

18 Student's own answers.

19 Student's own answers.

Writing: a longer piece of coninuous writing

20 Student's own answers.

21 Student's own answers.

22 Model answer.
Hi Sandy,
I'm really pleased you're coming to visit my country. The first place you should visit is London. It's one of the most famous cities in the world. It has fantastic museums and parks and is perfect if you like shopping. The buses and the underground are the best ways to travel.
After that you should go to the Lake District. I think this is the most beautiful part of England. It has the highest mountains in the country and the largest and deepest lakes. You can get there by train and then use the buses to get around.
Best wishes,
Martin

23 Student's own answers.

Grammar and Vocabulary Unit 6

1 1 F   2 G   3 B   4 E   5 J   6 A   7 D   8 H   9 C   10 I

2 1 train   2 department store 3 motorway   4 cafe   5 street
6 castle   7 airport

3 1 opposite   2 across   3 between   4 next to   5 behind
6 on your right   7 in front of   8 on your left

4 1 bored   2 new   3 favourite   4 full   5 careful   6 tired
7 healthy

5 1 comfortable   2 modern   3 friendly   4 interesting   5 old
6 high   7 famous

6 +*er/est* – clean, low, high, cheap, old, new, fast, strong
   more/the most … – expensive, modern, comfortable, difficult,
   important, careful, interesting, crowded

7 1 safer / faster 2 worse 3 cheaper 4 older 5 bigger
   6 earlier 7 prettier 8 thinner 9 better 10 further

8 1 more expensive 2 more interesting 3 hotter 4 prettier
   5 better 6 more excited 7 noisier 8 worse

9 1 the cheapest 2 the most 3 the largest 4 the most
   5 the most expensive 6 the smallest 7 the oldest

10 1 the best 2 cheaper 3 bigger 4 the largest
   5 the most interesting 6 the finest

UNIT 7   JOBS, WORK AND STUDY

Lead-in
1 1 C 2 D 3 A 4 B

Vocabulary: skills and abilities
2 1 A 2 I 3 F 4 D 5 G 6 B 7 J 8 H 9 E 10 C

Listening: note completion extension
4 Student's own answers.
5 1 chef 2 Wednesday 3 three / 3 4 8:00 / 8.00 / 8 o'clock
   5 sixteen / 16 6 maths 7 English 8 Italian 9 London
   10 Dinner with Jack 11 2004 12 2002 13 2005 14 two / 2

Grammar: *can / can't / could / couldn't*
6 Possible answers:
   1 At school, I was a really bad student. I couldn't understand maths
     easily and I couldn't write very well.
   2 When I was 16, I could only cook soup from a tin and I couldn't
     write a sentence without making lots of mistakes.
   3 Now, I can cook over 100 dishes and write books. I can't work for
     really long hours any more like I could at The Lemon Grove.
7 1 Jack can write books.   2 Jack can cook many types of food.
   3 Jack could cook only one type of food.   4 Jack can't work long hours.
   5 Jack couldn't understand maths easily.   6 Jack couldn't write well.
   7 Jack couldn't do well in exams.
8 1 can 2 can't 3 could 4 couldn't 5 couldn't 6 can

Speaking: describing skills and abilities
9 Student's own answers.
10 Student's own answers.
11 Student's own answers.

Vocabulary: work experience
12 1 video games designer 2 helping elderly people
   3 sports coach 4 lifeguard 5 sales assistant

Reading 1: true, false, not given
13 1 Gives people advice about jobs and careers.
   2 Explain how young people can use their summer holiday to get
   useful work experience.
14 1 It gives you the opportunity to earn money and gain useful work
   experience / learn new skills. It helps to find a job.   2 Five / 5
16 1 A 2 C 3 B 4 A 5 B 6 B 7 C 8 B
17 Student's own answers.

Writing: an email for a summer job
18 hotel receptionist
19

Feature	✓ ?
She says which job she is interested in	✓
She says what skills she has.	✓
She says what skills she didn't have in the past but does now.	
She uses a good structure – greeting to start the email and ends with her name	✓
She uses correct and appropriate grammar.	
She **only** talks about the information in the instructions	
She uses the correct number of words	✓

22 Student's own answers.

Grammar and Vocabulary Unit 7
1 1 F 2 B 3 G 4 J 5 E 6 A 7 D 8 C 9 H 10 I
2 1 passed 2 studying / finishes 3 get 4 taught
   5 learn / take 6 failed / take 7 started / learn 8 starting
3 1 receptionist 2 doctor 3 waiter 4 teacher 5 lifeguard
   6 shop assistant 7 cleaner 8 chef
4 1 experience 2 hard-working 3 long hours
   4 speak another language 5 friendly and helpful
   6 sports, art or music 7 energy 8 weekend
5 1 at 2 at 3 in/at 4 on 5 in / at 6 at 7 at
6 Restaurant – waiter, tables, chef, meal
   Hotel – receptionist, rooms, guests, lift, cleaner
   Shop – cash desk, clothes, changing rooms, shop assistant
7 1 Can you 2 I can 3 I can't 4 can you 5 I can
8 1 can 2 can't 3 couldn't 4 couldn't
9 1 ✗, can 2 ✓ 3 ✓ 4 ✗, Could they 5 ✓

UNIT 8   HEALTH AND MEDICINE

Lead-in
1 Student's own answers.

Listening 1: matching
2 1 to the sports centre 2 joining the gym
3 1 Samantha 2 Tom 3 Sarah 4 Samantha 5 Samantha
   and Sarah 6 Sarah

Vocabulary and speaking
4 1 eat fruit and vegetables 2 play basketball
   3 enjoy art and music 4 go cycling 5 play tennis
   6 drink water 7 watch TV 8 get enough sleep
5 Student's own answers.

Reading: an opinion based essay
6 watching TV go cycling play tennis get enough sleep
7 1 disagree
   2 The writer says that sports lessons make students healthier and
   help students feel less stressed.
9 1 C 2 B 3 B 4 A

Grammar 1: should / shouldn't / should not

10 1 bad 2 wants 3 not to go
12 1 should 2 should 3 shouldn't 4 should 5 shouldn't

Speaking: describing a picture

13 C B A

Vocabulary: how to relax

15 1 do exercise 2 drink tea 3 read a book 4 do yoga
  5 go for a walk

Listening 2: multiple-choice questions

16 1 read a book 2 do yoga 3 do exercise 4 go for a walk
  5 drink tea
17 1 C 2 B 3 A 4 B 5 A

Grammar 2: have to / don't have to

18 1 have to 2 don't have to 3 Do you have to 4 has to
  5 don't have to

Writing: an email to a friend giving advice

19 tennis and basketball
20 Student's own answer.
21 Student's own answer.

Grammar and Vocabulary Unit 8

1 1 go cycling 2 do yoga 3 play tennis 4 play basketball
  5 go for a walk 6 do exercise
2 1 join 2 drink / do 3 eat / do 4 go / get 5 have / get
  6 play / go 7 get 8 drink 9 play
3 1 Incorrect – What should you eat to be healthy? 2 Correct
  3 Incorrect – No, you shouldn't play on your computer for so long.
  4 Correct 5 Incorrect – I think you should try it.
4 1 should drink 2 should get 3 shouldn't watch 4 should play
  5 should ride 6 shouldn't eat
5 1 have to 2 have to 3 don't have to 4 don't have to 5 have to
  6 don't have to 7 have to 8 don't have to
6 1 have to / don't have to 2 don't have to / have to
7 1 should 2 should 3 should 4 should 5 shouldn't
  6 should
8 1 C 2 E 3 D 4 B 5 F 6 A

UNIT 9   LANGUAGE

Lead-in

1 1 use a dictionary 2 talk to people whose first language is English
  3 listen to songs in English 4 write an email to a friend 5 keep a
  vocabulary notebook 6 study with a teacher in a classroom
  7 watch videos online 8 read newspapers and magazines
2 Student's own answers.

Vocabulary and speaking

3 1 to 2 by 3 about 4 with 5 with
4 1 C 2 E 3 D 4 B 5 A
5 Student's own answers.

Grammar: *going to* for future plans

6 1 meet 2 video call 3 learn 4 study 5 send
7 1 The writer uses *going to*.
  2 tonight, this afternoon, next week, today, this morning, at the
  weekend
9 1 ✗, am going to 2 ✓ 3 ✓ 4 ✗, is going to buy
  5 ✗, Are you going to tell 6 ✓
10 Student's own answers.

Listening: discussing a language project

11 1 False 2 True 3 True
12 1 Student services 2 College office
  3 Student administration office 4 A

Speaking : a longer talk about a topic

13 Student's own answers.
14 Student's own answers.

Vocabulary and reading

15 1 C 2 B 3 C 4 A 5 B 6 C 7 C 8 B 9 A 10 B
16 1 He is an American teenager.
  2 He can hold a conversation in over twenty languages.
17 1 more / most 2 lots of 3 regularly
18 Student's own answers.

Reading: sentence completion

20 2 to another country 3 some work 4 their cultures
  5 West Africa 6 have fun

Writing: a short essay on a topic

21 Student's own answers.
22 Student's own answers.
23 Possible answer: C D A B / C A D B
25 1 C 2 B 3 C 4 C 5 A 6 A 7 A 8 B
26 1 Firstly 2 Furthermore 3 Additionally 4 On the other hand
  5 However 6 To sum up
27 Student's own answers.

Grammar and Vocabulary Unit 9

1 1 by 2 to / with 3 with 4 - 5 about 6 to / with 7 -
2 1 B 2 D 3 H 4 A 5 F 6 G 7 C 8 E
3 1 I'm not going to worry 2 Are you going to learn
  3 I'm going to try 4 Are you going to meet
  5 She isn't going to live
4 1 Who are you going to do the language project with?
  2 Where are you going to buy a dictionary from?
  3 How are you going to improve your language skills?
  4 When are you going to tell the teacher you want to move up to a
  higher level class?
  5 Why are you not going to go to university next year?
5 1 effort 2 work 3 advice 4 fun 5 time 6 skills
  7 progress 8 advantage
6 1 his English exam 2 advice 3 have fun 4 long time
  5 make any progress 6 English
7 make – a mistake dinner somebody laugh a noise
  a difference a guess
  take – a test an exam a picture a walk
8 1 am going to take 2 made 3 makes 4 take
  5 makes / making
9 1 Firstly 2 additionally/furthermore 3 Furthermore/Additionally
  4 However 5 To sum up
10 1 are going to have 2 are trying 3 discussed / were discussing
  4 communicates 5 to hold 6 had / am having / will have /
  am going to have

UNIT 10   SCIENCE AND TECHNOLOGY

Lead-in
1 1 smartphone 2 letter 3 laptop 4 tablet
   5 landline telephone 6 smart TV 7 smart watch
   8 desktop computer
2 Student's own answers.

Vocabulary and reading
3 1 crashed 2 shut down 3 websites 4 devices 5 network
4 1 attachments 2 download 3 stream 4 backup 5 store
5 B
6 1 different things 2 using a mail 3 sends information
   4 to go online 5 searching for information

Listening 1: a lecture
7 1 display 2 power button 3 input 4 microphone
   5 power bar 6 case
8 1 use an app 2 on or off 3 charge your phone, upload
   (some / your) files 4 speak into 5 check the battery
   6 protect the phone
9 1 38 2 62 3 78 4 86

Grammar and vocabualary
10 1 People 2 will 3 be 4 They 5 won't 6 look 7 Will
    8 they 9 look 10 What 11 will 12 smartphones 13 look
11 Student's own answer.
12 1 to rise 2 rose 3 to increase 4 an increase 5 to go up
    6 to fall 7 a fall 8 to decrease 9 decreased 10 went down
13 Answers in chart.

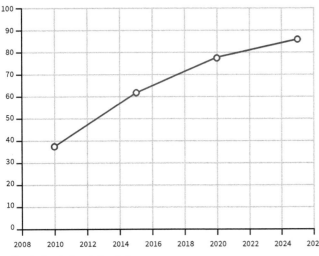

% of population with smartphones

14 1 B 2 A 3 C 4 B 5 A

Writing: describing a graph
15 Student's own answers.
16 Student's own answers.

Listening 2 and grammar
18 1 features 2 latest model 3 swipe 4 out of date 5 memory
19 1 D 2 C 3 E 4 A

Speaking: describing a gadget
20 Student's own answers.
21 Student's own answers.
22 Student's own answers.

Grammar and Vocabulary Unit 10
1 1 stores 2 network 3 laptop 4 Shut down
   5 apps / download
2 1 website 2 backup 3 device 4 attachment 5 crash
   6 stream
3 1 will communicate 2 won't be 3 Will the cars be able
   4 will people eat 5 will definitely need 6 will be
   7 will the animals breathe
4 1 y – from 2005 to 2010 2 (extra sentence)
   3 y – between 2010 and 2015 4 (extra sentence) 5 y – in 2030
   6 x 7 (extra sentence) 8 y – between 2020 and 2025
   9 y – between 2015 and 2020 10 (extra sentence)
5 1 increased 2 2005 3 55% 4 went 5 fall / decrease 6 down
   7 2020 8 rise 9 decrease / fall
6 A This is not the best summary. Firstly, it is not enough just to say
     that the lines 'went up and down a lot'. Second, it is not true to say
     that Line A 'changed much more than Line B', as both of them
     changed a great deal.
   B This is the best summary. The student has seen the difference in
     the main trends of Lines A and B, and has summarised this
     information well.
   C This is not the best summary. Too much detail, too many years and
     too many percentages are included. It is therefore not a summary.
7 1 I'm going to 2 latest model 3 out of date 4 features
   5 swiping 6 screen 7 memory 8 store 9 case

LISTENING SCRIPTS

UNIT 1   DAILY LIFE

Listening

16 and 17 ᴵᴵ▪ᴵ 02

Carlos: Hi Jack! I'm really excited about coming to stay with you at your house on the student exchange trip to Australia next term.

Jack: Me too, Carlos! I know you're going to have a great time at my school and with my family.

Carlos: Tell me a bit about your family. What do you all like doing?

Jack: Well, I love playing volleyball and basketball. I do volleyball once a week and basketball twice a week.

Carlos: I remember you have a brother. What does he do? Is he interested in sport, too?

Jack: No, not really. He prefers staying at home and reading. He's a member of our local gym but he never goes.

Carlos: Oh, that sounds like me! You've got a sister too, haven't you?

Jack: Yes, she's really good at painting and drawing. Some of her work is hanging up on the walls at home, so you'll be able to see it when you come.

Carlos: That would be great. I'd love to see it. What about your parents?

Jack: Well, my mum loves growing things. She spends a lot of time outdoors, planting flowers and cutting the grass.

Carlos: That sounds interesting. And your dad? What does he like doing?

Jack: Well, he's really good at building and fixing things. If anything gets broken around the house, he fixes it. He makes new things, too, like furniture.

Carlos: Great! And I know your grandma lives with you. What does she like doing?

Jack: Well, we're lucky – she's an amazing cook and makes us all wonderful meals every day. She already wants to know what you like eating.

Carlos: [Laughs] Really? Well, that gives me an idea for a present for her – a recipe book from where I'm from in the USA.

Jack: Perfect!

UNIT 2   HOUSE AND HOME

Listening 1

7 and 8 ᴵᴵ▪ᴵ 03

Giorgio: I'm excited about going to university, but I feel nervous about leaving my home, especially my bedroom. I like it a lot. My bed is very comfortable – I've got four big pillows. When I sit on my bed, if I look out of the window I can see the garden. I often do my homework at my desk and, to help me study, I sometimes turn on the lamp so I can see my notes and my course books better. When I want to relax, I usually play games on my phone, which I keep in the drawers next to my bed. I haven't got my own bathroom. I need to go down the hall if I want a shower or bath. However, I have got a sink where I brush my teeth every morning before I go to college. I have two posters: one is above my bed and the other one is next to the TV. What else? I don't like curtains very much, so I don't have them. At the window, I have a blind instead. I think it will be strange at first sleeping somewhere new but I'm sure I'll get used to it and I'll make it feel like home.

Listening 2

13 and 15 ᴵᴵ▪ᴵ 04

Andrew: Good afternoon, Prime Location Agency, Andrew Taylor speaking. Can I first check your student status?

Giorgio: Hello, yes, of course. My name's Giorgio Rossi and I will soon be a student at Brickbat University. I'm calling today to discuss where to live when I come to the UK to study at the university.

Andrew: Oh, hello, Giorgio. Thank you for your call, I have some questions for you. I hope that you don't mind. Can you speak English?

Giorgio: Yes, but I apologise if I make any mistakes.

Andrew: Don't worry. So, what do you want to study?

Giorgio: I'm not sure exactly, but something with engineering.

Andrew: First of all, where do you want to live – in a room on campus or in private accommodation?

Giorgio: I'm not sure. Can you give me some advice?

Andrew: Of course! Well, tell me a little about your personality and your preferences. Are you a sociable person?

Giorgio: Oh, yes, I am definitely sociable. I live with my parents at the moment. We have a big family and there are always lots of visitors.

Andrew: OK, that's great. Do you also like to sometimes have a quiet room to study in private?

Giorgio: Well, it depends on how I feel. I sometimes like to be sociable and other times, I prefer to study alone. Can I ask, where exactly the accommodation is?

Andrew: Well, if you live in a room on campus, it is very convenient for your studies, as you actually live in a building in the university. However, it's also noisy. There are hundreds of other students who also live there, and they often make lots of noise, but if you live in private accommodation you have a quiet life in a different part of the city with maybe one or two other students who are your housemates. Although, it often takes a long time to travel to university. What do you think?

Giorgio: It's a difficult decision. I want to make lots of new friends, but I also know that I need to work hard and study.

Andrew: OK, one final question. Meals. Would you prefer to live somewhere which is catered?

Giorgio: I'm not sure. What does *catered* mean?

Andrew: *Catered* means that all your food is included in the price of the accommodation. For example, if you decide to live on campus you can usually choose catered accommodation. That means that, for example, every day, you can go to the canteen for your breakfast, lunch or dinner, and it's always free. The other option is self-catered accommodation, where you can either cook at home or you can go out for all of your meals. However, you always have to pay for your food.

UNIT 3   HOBBIES, LEISURE AND ENTERTAINMENT

Listening

4 and 5 📊 05

Deon: Hey, Mark! Are you still interested in coming on a week's adventure holiday with me this summer?

Mark: Of course, but can we go in August? I can't do June or July because of college.

Deon: Yeah, sure! I guess we need to book soon. There's a company called *World Trek* that my friend told me about. He went on one of their cycling holidays last year, and loved it. There's lots of information on their website.

Mark: Really?

Deon: Yes – they do different kinds of adventure holidays. There's one by the sea with lots of water sports, and another in the forest where you can do hiking and cooking, and you learn how to cook outdoors. The one I like best is in the mountains. We can do things like climbing and white water rafting. What do you think?

Mark: That sounds amazing! Is it expensive?

Deon: So so – there's a special offer on at the moment. Normally the price is six hundred and fifty pounds, but if you book before Friday, it's five hundred pounds. The sailing holidays are eight hundred pounds, so it's not bad!

Mark: What does that include?

Deon: Transport, accommodation and our guide. We only have to pay for meals and drinks.

Mark: That's really good, isn't it? Let's book tonight! Shall I come to your place this evening around seven?

Deon: Can you come at eight? I've got a tennis lesson until seven thirty.

Mark: Yes, sure. See you then.

UNIT 4   TRAVEL AND HOLIDAYS

Listening

7 📊 06

Part 1

Presenter: Good afternoon everybody and welcome to the travel show. Today, I'm talking to Anna Cox from Cambridge, who has recently taken part in the Summer Cultural Exchange Programme. Good afternoon, Anna!

Anna: Good afternoon!

Presenter: Anna, where can students go on the Summer Cultural Exchange Programme?

Anna: Well, students can travel to France or Spain on a language exchange, or to the USA on a sports or music exchange. I didn't go to the USA because I'm not very good at sports. However, I study French and Spanish at school, so I had two options. I've been to France before, so I decided to go to Spain instead.

9 📊 07

Part 2

Presenter: Where did you stay on your summer cultural exchange programme?

Anna: I stayed with a host family in a small village just outside the city of Seville. Most people in the city live in apartments, but my host family lived in a big house. The family had a daughter who was my age called Carmen, so we had lots of fun together. We also visited Carmen's grandparents who live on a farm in the countryside. As I love animals, it was a really good experience for me.

Presenter: How wonderful! How long are exchange programmes usually?

Anna: Well, most of the language exchange programmes last for two weeks but the sports and music exchange programmes last for four weeks. If you go on a language exchange programme in August, you can go for three weeks because it's the school holidays. I went on a language exchange to Spain in July, so I could only stay for two weeks, unfortunately.

Presenter: Who can take part in the programme?

Anna: Well, there are some age requirements for the programme. You must be over the age of fourteen to take part in the language exchange programme and sixteen for the sports and music exchange programme. If you want to take part in the sports and music exchange programme, you have to be on a school sports team or play in the school orchestra. You can only take part in the language exchange programme if you study French or Spanish.

Presenter: I see – so would you recommend this programme to other students?

Anna: Yes, definitely. I had a great time staying with Carmen and her family. I felt a bit homesick when I first arrived, but they were so friendly and welcoming. Carmen spoke really good English, so I was worried that I wouldn't improve my Spanish, but I always tried to speak Spanish with her parents. My language skills have improved a little bit, but I think that it's better to stay for three weeks because you have more time to practise the language.

Presenter: The whole programme sounds really interesting, Anna – thank you for telling us about it.

UNIT 5   FOOD

Listening

7 , 8 and 9 📊 08

Mark: Hi, Jane.

Jane: Oh, hi Mark.

Mark: I'm really looking forward to the food festival. I love Chinese food and I hope our friends can come.

Jane: Well, I'm afraid most of them are busy.

Mark: What even Marco? He always says he has nothing to do and that he's interested in trying new food.

Jane: Mohammed says Marco has no money. Mohammed can't go because he is helping his flatmate decorate his room.

Mark: But the festival is free!

Jane: Yes, but we have to go there on the underground and I'm sure he'll want to buy some food when he's there.

Mark: Well, I don't have much money either, perhaps Pierre could lend him some. He's got a job and he *is* Marco's best friend.

Jane: Oh, Pierre can't come either.

Mark: Really? Is he at work? All he thinks about is work!

Jane: No, his parents are coming from France and he's going to show them around London … you know, Big Ben, Tower Bridge …

Mark: OK, what about Hang Yie? Her mother owns a Chinese restaurant, she must be interested.

Jane: She is, but she's going to help with the cooking for her family's party on the day we're going. I don't know about Lucy and Larissa though.

Mark: Well, I phoned Lucy, but her flatmate said she was on holiday in Italy and won't be back until the week after the festival.

Jane: I didn't even know she was on holiday. And Larissa?

Mark: She's got a really important exam, so she needs to prepare for it!

Jane: Well, it looks like it's just going to be you and me then. Not to worry. We'll take lots of photos to show everyone!

Vocabulary and listening

14 ◼09

Chef: Today, I'm going to show you how to make one of my favourite recipes. It's a type of food that's been popular for thousands of years. The Jiaozi or dumplings are beautiful and have the shape of a half-moon. You start by making them in a similar way to noodles. You need to make some dough first, but this is quite easy.

15 ◼10

Chef: OK, so what do you need to make the dumplings? First of all, you need to make the cases. These are the cases which you'll put the other ingredients in. To make the cases, you need to make the dough. Of course, you need flour for this. To make 20 cases, you'll need four cups of flour. Then, mix the flour with two cups of water. Don't forget to add some salt, but only a little to add some taste.

When you've mixed the ingredients, leave the dough for ten minutes in the bowl to make sure it's ready. You can make the filling to go inside the dough while you wait.

There are two main ingredients in the filling. Firstly, you have the cabbage. You need to chop this up finely and add it to another important ingredient, the meat. You can use any meat, but today I'm using lamb. Put the meat and cabbage together and mix it by hand. When it's mixed well, you can add some other ingredients. In China, people like to add spring onions to their dumplings and I do too! I'd like some seafood today, too, so I'm going to add some shrimps. Chop the spring onions and shrimps into small pieces and mix them together with the rest of the filling. To make sure that everything sticks together, add some vegetable oil.

Now that the mixture is ready, you need to finish the cases. First, cut the dough into twenty pieces, making sure they're all the same size, and roll them into flat little circular shapes. Put the mixture into the centre of the cases. Make sure you don't put too much filling in at this stage otherwise you won't be able to close the cases and all the filling will come out when it's cooking. Then, fold them into half-moon shapes. Finally, boil the dumplings three times, and there you have it. Delicious half-moon dumplings ready to eat.

UNIT 6   TRANSPORT AND PLACES IN TOWN

Listening

7 and 8 ◼11

Part 1

Presenter: Hello everyone and welcome to this talk about Northfields' Shopping Centre. It opens next weekend and I'm very excited to be able to tell you about it tonight. It's a beautiful building, full of light and colour and a wonderful place to spend time in. It was designed by a prize-winning architect – John Gadzen. That's G-A-D-Z-E-N. Have a look at his website – he's done some fantastic work.

Northfields is just outside town, on Forest Drive. If you're coming by car and want to use your sat nav, then the postcode is WT3 5BX. That's the easiest way to do it; it works better than using the address.

We are open seven days a week, and our opening hours are ten am until six pm every day except Thursday. That's when we have late-night shopping until 8:00 pm. We're planning to open late on Wednesdays too, but that won't happen until we see how popular the centre is.

There are lots of ways to get to us. We have a large car park, which at the moment is free to use. You can also come by bus from the town centre. Bus 635 brings you to the entrance. There's also bus 729, but that stops further away and it's a five-minute walk to the shopping centre. And of course, you can use the underground. A ticket from town is only £3.50. The bus costs £2.00, so the underground is a bit more expensive but much faster. From the town centre, it only takes fifteen minutes!

10 and 11 ◼12

Part 2

Presenter: OK, now let me show you a map of the shopping centre. As you can see, there are two floors. On the first floor there's a cinema, where you can see some great movies. And opposite that, in a smaller area, there are lots of places to eat and drink. There are fast-food restaurants as well, if you don't have time to sit and eat. All the shops are on the ground floor. The biggest shop is the supermarket. If you use the car park entrance, it's the last shop on your right. Then, all the way over on the other side of the building, is the second biggest shop – Green's department store. You can get almost anything in there, including gifts, things for the kitchen, and furniture.

Also on the ground floor is a pharmacy selling medicine, and health and beauty products. You'll find it between the men's and women's clothes shop and the café. Male and female toilets are also on this floor, which is on the same side as the cafe. There's also a great book store selling everything you might need for school. If you're coming from the car park entrance, that's the second shop on your right, next to the sports shop. Oh, and if you need a mobile phone, that's the smallest shop in the shopping centre – between the bank and the shoe shop. You can get all the latest mobile phones there. So I hope you'll all visit Northfields' soon and that you'll have a great time here!

UNIT 7   JOBS, WORK AND STUDY

Listening

5 ◼13

Jack: Good evening! Hello, my name's Jack Riley. I worked in a restaurant when I was younger, but now I'm a famous chef. You can listen to my cooking show on Mondays at half past seven. This Wednesday, you can see me on the TV show *Before They Were Famous*. I'm going to tell you about my life before I became a TV chef. You can see the programme on channel three and they will show it at eight o' clock.

People often ask me how I became so successful, and I tell them that it wasn't always that way. Most of my friends left school when they were eighteen and went to university, but I left school when I was sixteen. At school, I was a really bad student. I only passed my exams in History and French. I couldn't understand maths easily and I couldn't write very well, so I failed my exams in both maths and English.

I always enjoyed trying different foods, especially on holidays in Spain with my family, but I first discovered my love of cooking when I got a summer job working in the kitchen in an Italian restaurant near my home. The chefs there could make these amazing dishes out of really simple ingredients. I wanted to be like them, but I lived in a small village near Cambridge and it wasn't possible to train to be a chef there. I applied for jobs in Rome, but I couldn't speak Italian so in the end, I decided to move to London and train to be a chef.

Today, my career is more successful than I could have ever imagined. I first appeared on TV in *The Food Show* in 2005, and I started presenting my radio show, *Dinner with Jack* in 2006. I wrote my first bestselling cookbook, *Jack's Best Dishes* in 2004. And I worked as head chef at two top London restaurants: *The Olive Tree* in 2001, and *The Lemon Grove* between 2002 and 2005. I'm married with two beautiful children – and my third child will be born in December! When I was 16, I could only cook soup from a tin and I couldn't write a sentence without making lots of mistakes. Now, I can cook over 100 dishes and write books. I can't work for really long hours any more like I did at *The Lemon Grove*. That was the hardest I have ever worked in my life! And I still can't do maths!

UNIT 8 HEALTH AND MEDICINE

Listening 1

2 ▮▮ 14

Part 1

Samantha: Hello, Tom.

Sarah: Hi, Tom. Where are you going?

Tom: Hi, Sarah. Hi, Samantha. I'm going to the sports centre.

Sarah: Oh, great. I'm thinking of joining the gym there.

Tom: Really? Why don't you come with me and get some information about it?

3 ▮▮ 15

Part 2

Sarah: Ok, thanks. Did you join the gym?

Tom: Yes, I did. It's got really great equipment – all very modern and new. However, it is a little bit expensive – almost forty pounds a month, and that's with a student discount… But I've been every day since I joined.

Sarah: £40 a month! That *is* expensive. However, if you think it's a good gym, maybe I'll try it.

Samantha: Well, I think £40 a month is way too much. I don't know why people spend so much money on a gym membership, when they can exercise in the park for free.

Tom: I've tried running in the park, but it was really boring! I prefer to exercise with friends because it encourages me to work harder.

Sarah: I prefer to do exercise with friends as well – it's much more fun than exercising alone.

Samantha: But it's not just running. They have group exercise classes there in the park in the morning. Exercising outside is better because you get lots of fresh air. And you can exercise with a personal trainer, too.

Sarah: That sounds good. I think I'd like to have a personal trainer. How much does one cost?

Samantha: I pay £20 an hour.

Tom: £20 an hour! Doesn't that work out to be more expensive than joining the gym?

Samantha: It *is* expensive, but I think that it's worth the money. You can find out which type of exercise is best for you, and you can get some really useful advice on diet, too.

Sarah: That does sound useful. I need some advice on my diet – it's not great at the moment. And I know that a healthy diet helps you get fit.

Samantha: I can give you the email address of my personal trainer if you want.

Sarah: That's great! Thanks Samantha.

Tom: What about the gym? Do you think you'll join it?

Sarah: Yes – I think I'm going to try both.

Listening 2

16 and 17 ▮▮ 16

Jim: When I need to relax, I usually read a book. I believe that reading can also change your mood. For example, a good novel can make you forget about all of your worries and a funny story can make you feel happy. If you're feeling sad, you shouldn't read a sad story though, as this will make you feel worse.

Elena: For me, doing yoga is the best way to relax. You don't even have to spend a long time doing it to feel the benefits – even five minutes of breathing exercises can make a difference. Doing yoga will help you breathe deeply, which is the fastest way to feel more relaxed. You can do yoga classes in many different places. It isn't expensive either! Many sports centres offer yoga classes at a low price. You have to find a good teacher though – that's really important.

Kate: I think that doing regular exercise is the best way to relax. It's good for the body and also for the mind. After a short run or work out we feel more relaxed and happier. Often a person's reason for not doing regular exercise is they don't have enough time. However, you can always find ways to do more exercise, like walking instead of getting the bus or driving.

Mike: When I am feeling stressed at work, I go straight outdoors for a walk in the park. Breathing fresh air and looking at nature helps me to deal with my problems. Being active for just twenty minutes outside is enough to make you feel healthier, but the longer you spend, the better. I try to spend half an hour every day exercising during my lunch break. I can't spend the whole hour outside because I don't always have time. Everyone should give it a try.

Mark: When I want to relax, the first thing I do is make myself a cup of tea. I think green tea makes me feel calmer than black tea, but all types of tea can make you feel less stressed. A recent study found that people who drink tea during stressful times are much more relaxed than those who don't. You shouldn't drink tea at night though or you may find it difficult to sleep.

UNIT 9 LANGUAGE

Listening

11 and 12 ▮▮ 17

Sofia: Oliver, we need to discuss about how to start our project. Remember that our teacher wants us to write the report on two things. One, how many students in college already speak more than one language…

Oliver: … yes, and two, what level their English is. It's a big project so I think we're going to have to speak to a lot of people.

Sofia: Yes, I know! Do you really think it'll be possible to speak to everyone? I'm not sure. There are over two hundred students in total.

Oliver: I know, but I guess only half of them speak just a single language.

Sofia: That's still a lot. I don't think we have enough time to go around and have a chat with the whole college. How are we going to show the results?

Oliver: I think it'll be a problem if we only include numbers. We need more than that.

Sofia: Yes, I agree. Maybe including some graphs or tables is a good idea. Let me think… First, we need to find out how many students we have here in the college in total. Then we can work out how many of them speak two or more languages.

Oliver: Can I make a suggestion? I think we can ask for that information from the college office first. I remember that, on my first day here, I put information about my second language on the registration form. So, I think it's the same for everyone.

Sofia: That's a good idea. That'll save us some time. I'll make an appointment to go and speak to somebody there after class. Who do I need to see? Is it Miss Wainwright?

Oliver: No, she works in the student services room. You need to see Miss Smith. She's in the college office.

Sofia: Can you remind me where that is? Is it next door to the IT services offices where Mr Black works?

Oliver: No, Mr Black is in the student administration office so you need to go to the floor above.

Sofia: Oh, OK. I know where that is now.

Oliver: Great. OK, I'm going to have lunch. Do you want to join me?

Sofia: No, sorry, I can't. I need to study for my maths test. Enjoy your lunch. I'm going to study in the library. Bye!

UNIT 10   SCIENCE AND TECHNOLOGY

Listening 1

8 ▮▮▮ **18**

Part 1

Good morning, I'm here today to talk about the design and the success of smartphones. They are convenient, and they allow us to keep control of our lives. One important reason why I think smartphones are so successful is because of their simple, clean design. Of course, there are many different brands, but let's look at a common example on this picture.

First of all, on the front of the phone, we have the glass touch screen, also known as the display. It's very easy, you only need to press your finger on this when you want to use an app. Next, on the top right side of the smartphone, is the power button. You use this to turn the phone on or off again.

At the bottom, there is a USB input. This is where you plug in and charge your phone.

You can also connect to a laptop and upload your files and photos from your phone. You will see just above this is the microphone. Whenever you make a call, you speak into this. At the opposite end of the touch screen, you can see the power bar, which you can look at to check the battery. If the bar is low, you will need to plug it in and charge it again soon.

Around the phone on the outside, keeping all of this in place is the case – sometimes made from plastic, but now more often made of metal. Many people think that the reason for the case is so that they can have a different design and colour and make it more personal. Actually, every phone needs a good, strong case to protect the phone from breaking.

9 ▮▮▮ **19**

Part 2

Smartphones are becoming more popular every day, all around the world. In 2010, 38 percent of the world's population owned a smartphone. Most of these people were from developed areas of the world, like North America and Europe. Five years later, that figure was a lot higher. In 2015, 62 percent of all people had one. And, in the future, these amazing little devices will probably be even more popular. So popular that, by 2020, 78 percent of the population will own one, and by 2025 many scientists believe that this number will be even higher still. Not as high as 100%, but close. This is mostly because, in the less developed parts of the world, people will be richer than they are now. So, in that year, when 86 percent will own one, what will smartphones look like? Will they look the same as they do now? I'm afraid I can't say for sure, but I do know that they won't look the same as the one in the picture that we're looking at today.

Listening 2

17 and 19 ▮▮▮ **20**

1   It has a silver case, and the screen is bigger than most other smartphones.
    The display is also really clear. It's really light, and thin, it's got a lot of <u>memory</u>, and the battery lasts for a very long time.

2   It's very expensive, so before I buy it, I'm going to visit a mobile phone shop first, so I can try all the new <u>features</u>. But I'm definitely going to get it online in the end. I'm sure it will be cheaper.

3   The phone I have now, the Plus 5, is the <u>latest model</u> – it came out last year. But I think it will start to be really slow and seem <u>out of date</u> soon. The Plus 6 is even faster, and it's better for playing games and streaming things online, so that's why I'm going to get it as soon as I can.

4   I'm not sure if it will help me with everything. It won't do my homework for me if I <u>swipe</u> the screen, for example. But I think it will be helpful for some things. There's an app for writing a study plan, so I'm going to download that, anyway.

The authors and publishers would like to thank the following people for their work on this level of the Student's Book.

Sarah Jane Lewis for her editing and work on development of the materials

William Inge for his proof reading

Design and typeset by emc design.

Audio produced by Leon Chambers at The Soundhouse Studios, London.

The publishers would like to thank the following people for their input and work on the digital materials that accompany this level.

Nigel Barnsley; Lucy Passmore; Greg Sibley; Bryan Stephens

Cover and text design concept: Juice Creative Ltd.
Typesetting: emc design Ltd.
Cover illustration: MaryliaDesign/iStock/Getty Images Plus.

The authors and publishers acknowledge the following sources of copyright material and are grateful for the permissions granted. While every effort has been made, it has not always been possible to identify the sources of all the material used, or to trace all copyright holders. If any omissions are brought to our notice, we will be happy to include the appropriate acknowledgements on reprinting and in the next update to the digital edition, as applicable.

Key: B = Below, BL = Below Left, BR = Below Right, BC = Below Centre, C = Centre, CL = Centre Left, CR = Centre Right, L = Left, R = Right, T = Top, TR = Top Right, TL = Top Left.

Illustrations
Ana Djordjevic (Astound us) pp. 10, 15, 20, 36, 39, 40, 48, 58, 60, 62, 64, 69, 81, 90, 91, 96, 97, 100; Andrew Gibbs (Eye Candy Illustration) pp. 22, 73, 77, 79.

Photos
p. 10 (header): Caiaimage/Paul Bradbury/Caiaimage/GettyImages; p. 11: Christopher Futcher/Hemera/Getty Images Plus/GettyImages; p. 12 (TL): Rick Miller/Passage/GettyImages; p. 12 (BL): DMEPhotography/iStock/Getty Images Plus/GettyImages; p. 12 (CR): Henrik Trygg/Johner Images/GettyImages; p. 14: alvarez/E+/Getty Images Plus/GettyImages; p. 20 (header): Peter Cade/DigitalVision/GettyImages; p. 20 (photo 1): ultramarinfoto/E+/GettyImages; p. 20 (photo 2): hikesterson/iStock/Getty Images Plus/GettyImages; p. 20 (photo 3): daverhead/iStock/Getty Images Plus/GettyImages; p. 20 (photo 4), p. 28–29, p. 34 (BC): Westend61/GettyImages; p. 21 (curtain): dmitriymoroz/iStock/Getty Images Plus/GettyImages; p. 21 (lamp): bondrish/iStock/Getty Images Plus/GettyImages; p. 21 (TV): Tetra Images/GettyImages; p. 21 (desk): KatarzynaBialasiewicz/iStock/Getty Images Plus/GettyImages; p. 21 (shower): baona/E+/GettyImages; p. 21 (drawers): Glow Decor/Glow/GettyImages; p. 21 (window): Robert Warren/The Image Bank/GettyImages; p. 21 (poster): Glow Images/GettyImages; p. 21 (blinds): CBCK-Christine/iStock/Getty Images Plus/GettyImages; p. 21 (sink): Onzeg/iStock/Getty Images Plus/GettyImages; p. 21 (pillow): P.E. Reed/Photographer's Choice/GettyImages; p. 21 (cooker): gerenme/E+/GettyImages; p. 29: AlbertPego/iStock/Getty Images Plus/GettyImages; p. 31 (photo 1): ppart/iStock/Getty Images Plus/GettyImages; p. 31 (photo 2): ewg3D/E+/GettyImages; p. 31 (photo 3): Alphotographic/iStock Editorial/Getty Images Plus/GettyImages; p. 31 (photo 4): Jean-Yves Bruel/Photographer's Choice/GettyImages; p. 31 (photo 5): northlightimages/E+/GettyImages; p. 31 (photo 6): koosen/iStock/Getty Images Plus/GettyImages; p. 31 (photo 7): YangYin/E+/GettyImages; p. 31 (photo 8): Remus Moise/iStock Editorial/Getty Images Plus/GettyImages; p. 33: JackF/iStock/Getty Images Plus/GettyImages; p. 34 (header): Jupiterimages/Stone/GettyImages; p. 34 (TL): Seiya Kawamoto/DigitalVision/GettyImages; p. 34 (TC): Nick Daly/Cultura/GettyImages; p. 34 (TR): VisualCommunications/E+/GettyImages; p. 34 (BL): Georgijevic/iStock/Getty Images Plus/GettyImages; p. 34 (BR): Thorsten Jochim/Stock4B/GettyImages; p. 37 (BCL): andresr/E+/GettyImages; p. 36–37 (BL): martinedoucet/E+/GettyImages; p. 37 (CR): Caiaimage/Sam Edwards/Caiaimage/GettyImages; p. 37 (BCR): Dougal Waters/DigitalVision/GettyImages; p. 37 (BR): Hill Street Studios/Blend Images/GettyImages; p. 38 (L): Mike Marsland/WireImage/GettyImages; p. 38 (R): FRANCK FIFE/AFP/GettyImages; p. 40–41: Anadolu Agency/Anadolu Agency/GettyImages; p. 42: KatarzynaBialasiewicz/iStock/GettyImages; p. 43 (photo 1): Whit Preston/The Image Bank/GettyImages; p. 43 (photo 2): David Madison/The Image Bank/GettyImages; p. 43 (photo 3): Icon Sportswire/Icon Sportswire/GettyImages; p. 43 (photo 4): skynesher/E+/GettyImages; p. 43 (photo 5): BEN STANSALL/AFP/GettyImages; p. 43 (photo 6): Paul Bradbury/Caiaimage/GettyImages; p. 43 (photo 7): Arnold Media/The Image Bank/GettyImages; p. 43 (photo 8): NurPhoto/NurPhoto/GettyImages; p. 43 (photo 9), p. 115: mbbirdy/E+/GettyImages; p. 43 (photo 10): Bernard van Dierendonck/LOOK-foto/LOOK/GettyImages; p. 47 (header): Grafner/iStock/Getty Images Plus/GettyImages; p. 47 (CL): Kelly Loughlin Photography/Moment/GettyImages; p. 47 (CR): Hill Street Studios/Blend Images/Getty Images Plus/GettyImages; p. 47 (BL): Ariel Skelley/Blend Images/Getty Images Plus/GettyImages; p. 47 (BR): VisitBritain/VisitBritain/GettyImages; p. 58 (header): g-stockstudio/iStock/Getty Images Plus/GettyImages; p. 59 (TL): Henry Donald/Moment/GettyImages; p. 59 (TC): Fred Duval/FilmMagic/GettyImages; p. 59 (TR): FREDERIC J. BROWN/AFP/GettyImages; p. 59 (CL), p. 83 (photo 3): Hero Images/Hero Images/GettyImages; p. 59 (CR): kali9/E+/GettyImages; p. 59 (B): Robert Mullan/Canopy/GettyImages; p. 61 (photo 1): nino-p/iStock/GettyImages; p. 61 (photo 2): Kristin Lee/GettyImages; p. 61 (photo 3): Dorling Kindersley/Dorling Kindersley/GettyImages; p. 61 (photo 4): Laurence Mouton/Canopy/GettyImages; p. 61 (photo 5): anamejia18/iStock/Getty Images Plus/GettyImages; p. 61 (photo 6): NRedmond/iStock/Getty Images Plus/GettyImages; p. 61 (photo 7): Kanawa_Studio/iStock/Getty Images Plus/GettyImages; p. 61 (photo A): vvlado/iStock/Getty Images Plus/GettyImages; p. 61 (photo B): Sino Images/Sino Images/GettyImages; p. 61 (photo C): Thanh Nguyen/EyeEm/GettyImages; p. 63 (L): chengyuzheng/iStock/Getty Images Plus/GettyImages; p. 63 (C): Megan Danjul/EyeEm/EyeEm/GettyImages; p. 63 (R): Andrew Bret Wallis/Photodisc/GettyImages; p. 66 (photo 1): Allison Dinner/StockFood Creative/GettyImages; p. 66 (photo 2): vip2014/Moment Open/GettyImages; p. 66 (photo 3): Sarka Babicka/Moment/GettyImages; p. 66 (photo 4): Henrik Freek/StockFood Creative/GettyImages; p. 66 (photo 5): MAIKA 777/Moment/GettyImages; p. 66 (photo 6): James Worrell/Photonica/GettyImages; p. 66 (photo 7): James And James/Photolibrary/GettyImages; p. 66 (photo 8): Ian O'Leary/Dorling Kindersley/GettyImages; p. 70 (header): Rustam Azmi/Getty Images News/GettyImages; p. 70 (CL): Chad Ehlers/Photographer's Choice/GettyImages; p. 70 (C): GOH CHAI HIN/AFP/GettyImages; p. 70 (CR): TriggerPhoto/iStock/Getty Images Plus/GettyImages; p. 70 (BL): RudyBalasko/iStock Editorial/Getty Images Plus/GettyImages; p. 70 (BR): Martin Ruegner/Photolibrary/GettyImages; p. 74–75: Daniel Hopkinson/Arcaid Images/Arcaid Images/GettyImages; p. 80 (header): demaerre/Getty Images Plus/GettyImages; p. 80 (CL): BraunS/E+/GettyImages; p. 80 (CR): Marc Romanelli/Blend Images/GettyImages; p. 80 (BL): FredFroese/E+/GettyImages; p. 80 (BR): Monty Rakusen/Cultura/GettyImages; p. 83 (photo 1): Edge Magazine/Future/GettyImages; p. 83 (photo 2): MachineHeadz/iStock/Getty Images Plus/GettyImages; p. 83 (photo 4): PeskyMonkey/iStock/Getty Images Plus/GettyImages; p. 83 (photo 5): sturti/iStock/Getty Images Plus/GettyImages; p. 84 (R): Hybrid Images/Cultura/GettyImages; p. 84 (L): SilviaJansen/iStock/Getty Images Plus/GettyImages; p. 85 (T): Maskot/Maskot/GettyImages; p. 85 (C): James Braund/Lonely Planet Images/GettyImages; p. 85 (B): Panama7/Stock Editorial/Getty Images Plus/GettyImages; p. 92 (header): Ross Woodhall/Cultura/GettyImages; p. 92 (L): skynesher/iStock/Getty Images Plus/GettyImages; p. 92 (R): Martin Barraud/OJO Images/GettyImages; p. 98 (photo 1): Nick Dolding/Stone/GettyImages; p. 98 (photo 2): Morsa Images/Iconica/GettyImages; p. 98 (photo 3): Mike Chick/Stone/GettyImages; p. 98 (photo 4): Kelvin Murray/Stone/GettyImages; p. 98 (photo 5): Michael Blann/Iconica/GettyImages; p. 103 (header): Plume Creative/DigitalVision/GettyImages; p. 103 (photo 1): Godong/Photolibrary/GettyImages; p. 103 (photo 2): gmast3r/iStock/Getty Images Plus/GettyImages; p. 103 (photo 3): Westend61/GettyImages; p. 103 (photo 4): mihailomilovanovic/E+/GettyImages; p. 103 (photo 5): tommaso79/iStock/Getty Images Plus/GettyImages; p. 103 (photo 6): Spencer Grant/Photolibrary/GettyImages; p. 103 (photo 7): fizkes/iStock/Getty Images Plus/GettyImages; p. 103 (photo 8): Ghislain & Marie David de Lossy/The Image Bank/GettyImages; p. 107: Ian McKinnell/Photographer's Choice/GettyImages; p. 114 (header): Bloomberg/Bloomberg/GettyImages; p. 114 (photo 1): Jeffrey Coolidge/DigitalVision/GettyImages; p. 114 (photo 2): Maica/E+/GettyImages; p. 114 (photo 3): eestingnef/iStock/Getty Images Plus/GettyImages; p. 114 (photo 4): akova/iStock/Getty Images Plus/GettyImages; p. 114 (photo 5): code6d/E+/GettyImages; p. 114 (photo 6): pictafolio/E+/GettyImages; p. 114 (photo 7): koya79/iStock/Getty Images Plus/GettyImages; p. 114 (photo 8): adventtr/iStock/Getty Images Plus/GettyImages; p. 120: Stock/Getty Images Plus/GettyImages.